A Memoir
Of All Seasons

Sally Asenbrener Stejskal

Enjoy the read all about me!

Sally J Stejskal
August 2019

TGW

First Edition
August 2019

Book design and typesetting by
John Boswell Hudson & Sandra Cermak Hudson

Front cover image is of Sally Asenbrener Stejskal
Back cover image is of Blake Stejskal

Text is 12 pt Times New Roman

ISBN: 9781078436083
Imprint: Independently published

DEDICATION

This book is dedicated to my children, my grandchildren—
so they may know me better—and to my husband who has
supported both my career, and my decisions over the years,
some good and some not so good. I love you all. SAS

Grandsons Blake Stejskal, Ethan Cohen, Joseph Cohen
and Granddaughter Sydney Cohen

Table of Contents

Acknowledgements

Thanks to my fellow members of The Guild Writers of the National Czech & Slovak Museum & Library for their inspiration, encouragement, and guidance as I put a few memories to paper. I have enjoyed our group's fortnightly gatherings as we listen and critique one another's stories.

A special thanks to Carole Michalek Gauger, John Boswell Hudson, Sandra Cermak Hudson, Helga C.W. Mayhew, Mary Henkels Rhiner, and Anneliese Heider Tisdale for taking time out of their busy lives to help edit and design this book.

Also a special thanks to my friend, Linda Koehler, for reading my stories and making recommendations for improvement, and Patti Thacker for the cover photo of me.

Most sincerely, Sally Asenbrener Stejskal

Family Lines

Schlueter / Asenbrener family line:

Sally's maternal grandparents:
> Agnes Yearsa Schlueter & Charles Schlueter

Sally's paternal grandparents:
> Tillie Chabal Asenbrener & Vaclav Asenbrener

Sally's Parents:
> Mamie Schlueter Asenbrener & Leo Asenbrener
>> **Sally Asenbrener [Kenneth Stejskal]**
>>> Brent Stejskal [Lisa Glover]
>>> Blake Stejskal
>>> Lynette Stejskal [Russell Cohen]
>>>> Sydney Cohen
>>>> Joseph Cohen
>>>> Ethan Cohen
>>> Sandra Asenbrener [Kenneth Sonka]
>>> Lisa Sonka [James Young]
>>>> Jason Young
>>>> Karli Young
>>> Lori Sonka [Ed Carnvale]
>>>> Kevin Carnvale
>>>> Corey Carnvale

Svoboda / Stejskal family line:

Ken's maternal grandparents:
> Mary Merta Svoboda & Thomas Svoboda

Ken's paternal grandparents:
> Agnes Horusicka Stejskal & Joseph Stejskal

Ken's parents:
> Evelyn Svoboda Stejskal & Joseph Stejskal
>> **Kenneth Stejskal [Sally Asenbrener]**
>>> Lynette Stejskal [Russell Cohen]
>>>> Sydney Cohen
>>>> Joseph Cohen
>>>> Ethan Cohen
>>> Brent Stejskal [Lisa Glover]
>>> Blake Stejskal
>>> Kathy Stejskal O'Neil [Brian O'Neil]
>>>> Mallory O'Neil [Matt Heger]
>>>>> Lucy Heger
>>>>> Audrey Heger
>>>>> Frankie Rose Heger

Current generation photos

"As I reminisce, my memories of family grow fonder and fonder."

Asenbrener side of the family in 2016
Back row (L-R) James Young, Karli Young, Lisa Sonka Young, Lisa Glover Stejskal, Brent Stejskal, Sydney Cohen, Lynette Stejskal Cohen, Russell Cohen, Lori Sonka Carnvale, Corey Carnvale, Kevin Carnvale. Middle row center-Blake Stejskal
Front Row left to right—Jason Young, Sandra Sonka , Ken Stejskal, Sally Stejskal, Ethan Cohen, Joseph Cohen.

Stejskal side of the family in 2016
Back row (L-R)Audrey Heger, held by her mother Mallory O'Neil, Matt Heger, Kathy Stejskal O'Neil, Brian O'Neil. Russell Cohen, Lynette Stejskal Cohen, Sydney Cohen, Brent Stejskal, Lisa Glover Stejskal, Blake Stejskal,
Front row (L-R) Ken Stejskal with Lucy Heger in front of him, Sally Asenbrener Stejskal, Ethan Cohen, Joseph Cohen

FAMILY

Family is, and always has been, the most important part of my life. My mother had five brothers and sisters and my dad had three. Although we did not spend a lot of time with my dad's Asenbrener side of the family. We certainly did with my mother's Schlueter side of the family.

The Schlueter line had get-togethers for all major holidays, birthday celebrations, and most any reason to spend a Sunday or special day together for a family feast. Family reunions were held each year, one for the my maternal grandmother's side of the family and one for my paternal grandfather's.

Schlueter Family Reunion 1954
Sally is in the fourth row. She is the girl in the white dress with the long curls. Sandra is in the front row second from the left.

My Entry into the World

A slight breeze was blowing and there was the smell of burning leaves in the air. It was a beautiful fall day in Iowa. The date was September 20, 1941, and a bundle of joy was born to Mamie and Leo Asenbrener.

Mamie was the daughter of Charles and Agnes Schlueter and had two brothers and three sisters. They grew up on a farm near Amana, Iowa, and Mamie left the family home as a young girl after the eighth grade to make her way in the world as a helper in the house of wealthy families in Cedar Rapids.

She had many friends and happily danced to the Charleston and celebrated the weekends or her time off doing what young people did during the roaring twenties. She was considered a flapper, along with her friends, since they became part of a new breed of thinking and behavior during that period of history.

Mamie was saving her money to travel to Europe with her best friend, but a boyfriend named Leo Asenbrener convinced her to marry him instead, and buy a house with the money she had saved. This was the same home I grew up in, and where Mamie and Leo lived until their deaths.

Mamie on the left with her best friend, Alta

Mamie Schlueter Asenbrener & Leo Asenbrener

The bride and groom were attended by Mamie's sister
Gladys Schlueter Hrdlicka, and her husband Louis Hrdlicka.

Leo was the son of Vaclav and Tillie Asenbrener. He had one older brother and two younger sisters. His mother's maiden name was Chabal and they were originally from the Solon, Iowa area. There is a street named Chabal in Solon, but I have not investigated its family significance. Mamie and Leo were married on July 3, 1934.

Announcement of my mother's pregnancy and ultimately my birth created a lot of celebrating by family and friends since Leo and Mamie had been married for over seven years. Most newlyweds in that era started families soon after the wedding so people had long given up counting the months on their fingers since the wedding and were excited by the news of a new baby in the family.

I came into this world, like I guess most babies do, expecting the best. The war was going on in Europe, but it wasn't until December 7, 1941, with the attack on Pearl Harbor that caused everyone to take notice and keep tuned in to the newspapers and radio. Young men were being notified of their draft status and families were preparing to send them off to war. My father was not one of those young men waiting for his number to be called because on October 30, 1941, six weeks after my birth, he was driving home after a drinking session with buddies and had an automobile accident, not with another car, but a serious one for him and his car. His leg was badly crushed along with other serious injuries which hospitalized him for over six months. After all the surgeries and putting his leg back together, he walked with a limp and one leg shorter than the other for the rest of his life. I remember one shoe always having a built up sole to compensate for the difference.

During my dad's recovery period, my mother and I visited him at the hospital almost daily—first in Cedar Rapids at St Luke's Hospital and then later he was transferred to the University Hospitals in Iowa City. When he was released to come home, he was in a total body cast so moving around

5

much was almost impossible. Most of his time was spent in bed until the cast was removed and replaced with one just on his leg which allowed more mobility with the use of crutches. This was a difficult time in the life of my parents. Mother had to find a better paying job to help support us so she became employed at Wilson & Company, the local packing house. This was not an ideal job for my mother, but the pay was good. I was taken to my paternal grandparent's house to be cared for until my father was physically able to watch over me.

My father was released from the hospital in April 1942, but it would be several more months before he became mobile and could walk again. Our house was located on the south edge of Cedar Rapids close to an open field and about a block from railroad tracks. I was almost three years old when my father was finally able to care for me. We would sit outdoors below the big walnut tree in the back yard and pass the time of day away while my mother worked.

My dad with me at six months old

Since we were close to the railroad tracks, the railroad vagrants or bums as we called them quickly learned about my father being home with his little girl, so they would come to visit and collect a meal or some kind of drink. They were always pleasant and appreciative of whatever my father gave them. Oh, the stories they used to tell about riding the rails and sometimes they would leave a little gift or trinket for our hospitality. We got to know some of them quite well as they passed through often enough to stop on almost a regular schedule. When my father was finally able to return to work, my mother kept working at her job and I continued going to my paternal grandparents so the vagrants stopped coming.

The Asenbrener Family

My Deda Vaclav Asenbrener, dad's brother Lumir Asenbrener, an unidentified person, my dad Leo Asenbrener and In front, my Baba Tillie Chabal Asenbrener.

Baba Tillie Chabal Asenbrener holding six week old Sally

Each morning my mom would drop me off at my paternal grandparents on her way to work. My dad's parents, Tillie and Vaclav Asenbrener, were referred to as Baba *(bah bah)* and Deda *(juh da)*. As I read this story to my writers group, some of the Czech writers questioned my use of the name, Baba. A common meaning of the Czech word Baba is "old lady," but that is how she was known to me. My grandparents spoke mostly Czech, so when I began talking, I learned to speak Czech as well as English. Although I have forgotten most of the Czech language, I understand enough so you cannot talk about me behind my back.

Baba and Deda lived in a story and half house in Cedar Rapids close to Wilson School. Their house was not very modern and I remember it as being dark and dingy inside. It was heated by a huge coal-burning furnace in the basement. There was a steel floor-grate between the dining and living room to let the warm air escape into the living part of the house. The space below the grate was black and scary for a little girl, so I always avoided walking on it. Sometimes I would kneel down by the edge and peer into it to see if there was anything I could see down there. I was very careful not to drop any of my toys between the pattern of the grates or they would be lost forever.

A woodburning stove in the kitchen provided heat for that area and that is where we spent the most time. My Baba washed their clothes in a metal tub with a washboard using homemade soap. I would sit on the old wooden steps to the basement watching her scrub those clothes on the washboard—rub-a-dub-dub. The clothes were then hung outside on a metal clothesline. You had to wipe it off first to remove any dirt, and then you clipped the clothes to the line using wooden clothespins.

The old wooden washboard, tub, and clothespin

In the winter, the clothes on the line would freeze stiff as they dried. Your fingers felt like they were freezing stiff too. The clothes were always dried outdoors unless the weather was too bad. Then they had to be draped over racks and lines in the basement.

Ironing clothes was performed by heating a heavy iron on the woodburning stove in the kitchen until it was hot enough to use for pressing. Before ironing, the clothes were often sprinkled with water from a pop bottle with a cork sprinkler top and rolled up to dampen them before ironing.

Old fashioned iron had to be heated on a stove

Pop bottle and sprinkler top

This was a very tedious job, especially if the items were cotton garments that had been starched. When the iron cooled down it would be put back on the stove to heat up again. This process had to be performed over and over again, so you can understand what a dreaded job it was and the amount of time expended.

Baba and Deda's backyard extended to the middle of the block and contained a big garden and raspberry bushes all across the back. There was a cut through to the house behind them which we would walk through to visit with the neighbors. There was lots of shade in the backyard due to an abundance of trees, some of which were hickory nut trees. We would pick up the nuts in the fall, crack open the shells, and then spread them out on the kitchen table. We spent hours picking the nutmeats out of the shells to save for future baking. I thought this was a boring job and one which I quickly tired of. I was never very good at monotonous and repetitive tasks, which is probably why I enjoyed supervisory positions the most.

Time passed with day after day being pretty much the same until one day in 1948, something terrible happened. My Deda got sick and they took him to the hospital. I was scared and didn't understand what happened in hospitals. All I knew was that he never came home. He had died from a ruptured appendix.

All of my father's family and friends were very upset, and many were crying. People got dressed up in their best clothes, mostly in dark colors. There was a black wreath hung on the door of Baba and Deda's house and we went to a place called a funeral home. My Deda, very stiff looking, was lying in this strange box dressed in his Sunday suit. We were sitting in a special little room listening to a minister talk about my Deda. There was organ music playing sad songs and a lot of praying. No one was paying attention to this seven-year-old girl. I remember looking out the window of this long black car on the way to the cemetery feeling very much alone and frightened. Death was a very scary experience for me and I couldn't wait for those feelings to pass and to feel happy again.

11

People brought food to Baba's house and congregated there after the burial with many stories being told and some laughter. All that didn't help me get rid of the sadness.

Nothing was the same after Deda died. My Baba's health was such that she couldn't live alone in their house. A new garage was moved onto our property and converted into a little house for her. It consisted of two rooms but it was comfortable for her and gave her a bit of privacy. It did not have plumbing, so she used the outdoor toilet and took her showers in our house. Most of the time she ate her meals with us. She did have a little hot plate she could warm things up on when she didn't want to go out. She had never learned to drive so my mom was the one to usually take her places— mostly doctor appointments.

I recall her not having any teeth, which was a curiosity for me and my friends, so a dentist was not one of her needs. In spite of not having any teeth, I remember she could eat and chew any kind of food. Baba was a big lady and weighed over 300 pounds. She had long silver grey hair which she twisted into a bun on top of her head. I don't remember her taking it down to comb very often, and I doubt it got washed very often either. Her weight contributed to a lot of health issues for her and was an ultimate cause of her death. This happened within a year after she moved in with us. I remember having those same scary thoughts as we went through the funeral business again. The black wreath was on our house this time. It took several days for me to get over all those sad feelings again. It was several years into adulthood before I could face going to anyone's funeral, unless I absolutely had to.

More About Dad

The circus is in town—the circus is in town. We lived close enough to Hawkeye Downs, the event center of my early years, so we knew when the *All Iowa Fair* was in progress. We could hear the roar of the stock cars or midgets racing, and we could see the big Fourth of July fireworks show from our front yard. Having the circus in town was a really special event and very exciting.

Dad promised to take me, and one of my little school friends, after he got home from work on a Friday evening. He always got paid on Friday. I couldn't believe it because it was very rare that we could afford to attend such events. Friday night came. We waited and waited for Dad to come home. Darkness fell and it became later and later. Finally Dad came home and said we would go. We jumped into our old car and off we went.

We parked in a field that did not have a charge for parking and walked across the street to the entrance to the circus tent. Jumping up and down with excitement while Dad went up to the ticket seller, he quickly returned and informed us he did not have enough money to get in. He had spent his extra money at the tavern on his way home.

We had to be satisfied walking around the grounds hearing the music and people clapping during the show. We felt the excitement and were able to see the elephants staked outside the "big top." That was quite an experience, even though it was another night of disappointment for a little six-year-old to remember.

So if you think my father was a mean or cold-hearted man, he wasn't. He cared about his family, was easy going, and a hard worker. He grew up on a farm near Solon, Iowa, where his family lost everything they owned during the Great Depression. His family was forced to move to town, which was Cedar Rapids. The men were lucky to find employment during such hard times. My father was not an educated man, and was suitable for only blue collar jobs. He was hired by Weaver Witwer, owner of Witwer Grocer Company.

Mr. Witwer owned and operated a chain of grocery stores, a food processing plant and warehouse, thirty-two farms with the latest equipment, and a fleet of red trucks. The trucks were seen all across the Midwest delivering groceries to his stores known as *Me Too*. My dad worked hard on the dock, loading and unloading trucks. He was paid very little for his efforts, which probably is what made Mr. Witwer so successful.

Pay day was on Friday. Several of the employees' wives and families met after work to cash their pay checks on "the avenue," now known as *Czech Village*. They bought their groceries at the *Me Too*. After loading them into their cars, the wives joined their husbands at the favorite tavern for a few beers, a chance to listen to live music, usually an accordion or concertina player. The kids played shuffleboard and drank pop.

What fun we had until a local ordinance was passed that did not allow children in bars. This was upsetting to our group of families, but we continued our weekly merriment. The children were either left in the cars to wait until their parents returned, or if lucky, given money to go to either one of the drug stores for a comic book, ice cream—or if really lucky, a hamburger and malt at *Cyclone's*, an old boxcar converted to a diner at the end of the street.

Mr. Witwer's success continued to grow. Next to his warehouse he built a five-story building, now known as the *Bottleworks Loft Condominiums*. I used to stand outside the main-floor row of large windows, and watch the gleaming display of equipment creating beverages on the assembly line of the bottling works. It was a special treat when Dad brought home a case of pop branded *Life,* which came in

14

many different flavors. Those windows are still there today, currently looking into a beauty salon.

Mr. Witwer's success also allowed him to build an opulent Georgian-style home and stable known as *Hilltop Farm* off East Post Road SE. One summer he hosted a picnic

there for all his employees and their families. My sister and I were very excited about visiting this stately mansion on the hill. I remember the tables set out on the beautiful green lawn were covered with white tablecloths. There was an abundance of food and beverages. What sticks in my memory the most, as a seven-year-old, was that all the people doing the serving were black. This was a whole new experience for me. To this day I remember what a shock that was. I thought all black people lived in the south and worked on cotton plantations.

I believe my dad resented Mr. Witwer's success resulting from the paltry wages he paid his employees. So when Dad came home after work with a bottle of Betty Ann Port, a very inexpensive wine, he would sit at the kitchen table drinking and ranting and raving about Mr. Witwer. It didn't matter if anyone was listening or not. Dad never got mean, just loud in his expression of dislike for his boss. Dad's tirade would go on for hours! My sister and I pulled the covers over our head and tried to block out the noise coming from the kitchen. My mother would often try to convince him to come to bed, but usually to no avail. He just had to talk himself out, and then take himself to bed.

I often accompanied my dad to the state-run liquor store to buy his wine. He had to write his order from a list of available liquor posted on the wall. The order was then given to a clerk, who retrieved the liquor from behind the counter, and recorded Dad's purchase in his personal purchase book. The state kept track of how much liquor each individual bought. They say it was a custom for parents to inspect the purchase books of their children's suitors to determine their drinking habits.

Up until the day of his retirement, I don't remember my dad ever missing a day of work, regardless of weather or illness. Right before he retired, union representatives came into Mr. Witwer's operation and organized the labor force. Finally, a decent wage was paid to the workers.

I believe my dad's heart was always with farming. When he had to give up his early dream of owning his own farm, and instead had to work at a job he so disliked, seemed to be a very good reason why he often turned to alcohol. My dad's dream after retirement was to buy a fishing boat and spend leisurely days on the river with a rod and reel. That never happened, since illness and ultimately death occurred shortly after he turned sixty-five.

The Schlueter Family

Grandparents, Charles and Agnes Yearsa Schlueter, with their six children from left to right: my mother Mamie Asenbrener, Wilma Benish, Walter, Frank ,Lillian Vorel, and Gladys Hrdlicka.

I need to talk a little about my mother's side of the family. She was the daughter of Agnes Yearsa Schlueter and Charles Schlueter. The Schlueter side of the family played a major role in my life, shaping my thoughts and nurturing my abilities. As I grew up, Mother became my best friend. I still miss her even after these many years since her death in 1969. She was a very hard worker, trying to do her best for her family

17

while putting up with an alcoholic husband. I don't remember her complaining about anything that life dealt her, including her last days on earth losing her battle with cancer.

Mother was one of six kids growing up on a farm by the Amanas. Her father was German and her mother was Czech, although they both spoke Czech. She had two brothers and three sisters.

Let me introduce my mother's siblings. Her sister, Wilma, was a farmer's wife, married to Edwin. They had four children—three girls, Donna, Bonnie, Judy, and a boy, Donald. Wilma was responsible for the home, meals, laundry, garden, and raising chickens. As soon as the children were old enough various chores were assigned to them. Aunt Wilma lived to celebrate her 100th birthday, passing on the next day.

Mother's brother, Walter, spent his working years as a millwright for the local packing house, *Wilson & Co.* He and his wife, Helen, never had children. They enjoyed their nieces and nephews, and spent leisure time traveling and taking care of their home. He was an excellent wood craftsman, building many beautiful things including my corner hutch and my grandfather clock.

Brother Frank was a scholar. He studied education and teaching, later becoming a mortician, and then went back to teaching. His first wife, who I never knew, passed away with the birth of their first child, a baby girl. My grandparents helped raise Janice until Frank remarried. His second wife, Henrietta, gave birth to two more children, another daughter, Paula, and a son, Rich.

Lillian was the sister dearest to my mother, and my fondest aunt in later years. She was the right hand of her husband, Milo, helping him with whatever endeavors he chose to attempt, whether it be farming, home building, or sales in a lumber yard. Their pride and joy was in their only child, a daughter, Nancy.

18

Gladys was the youngest sister. She was another farm wife, supporting her husband, Louis, as they raised livestock and numerous crops. They had only one daughter, Linda.

All of my aunts and uncles lived into their mid or late nineties, enjoying life to the fullest.

Family was very important, and every holiday, birthday or special occasion was spent going back to my maternal grandparents' farm for a huge dinner and get-together. Everyone brought food to share. The main dish was prepared by my Babi and often included freshly butchered chickens fried to perfection.

She butchered her chickens early in the morning by placing them on an old stump behind the house, and chopping their heads off with a hatchet. She then plunged them into boiling hot water to make it easy to remove the feathers. Next the innards were removed. This process produced an awful smell I will never forget!

Babi cooked and baked on an old wood-fired stove in the big kitchen where everybody gathered. I can still smell the wonderful fragrances now coming from that kitchen before each meal. The biggest meal of the day was at noon. However, we snacked all afternoon, and before returning home, took something to eat on the way, or for the next day.

We would leave for the farm in our old Ford Model A early in the morning. Since we lived in Cedar Rapids, going to the farm was a major trip, especially with the old car not being the most reliable. A tire pump was always carried along since flats were a common occurrence. Sometimes the radiator would boil over so we had to stop to let it cool down and add water. In winter, blankets were a necessity to keep warm. It was always an adventure going to the farm. Even after our cars were upgraded, it still remained an adventure.

Sally waiting to leave in the old car

Once we arrived at the gate to the long lane leading to the farm, I could barely contain my excitement. All the cousins would be there and we never lacked for something to do. Boredom was an unknown word in our vocabulary, since we could explore all the outbuildings on the farm in good weather. There was the machine shed full of rusty old pieces of equipment to climb on, since Deda no longer farmed the land. There was the chicken house to check for eggs, even though they had already been gathered in the morning, and the corn crib filled with corn cobs to build imaginary things with. Then there was the hog pen. It was always fun to climb up on the gate and watch the pigs wallow in the mud or eat the garbage given to them.

View of the farm from the lane leading from the gravel road

The big old red barn was also a special place to visit. There were cats and kittens darting about hissing at us if we got too close, since they were too wild to catch, and only came out for food. As we grew older, it was a great place to take our BB guns and shoot at the pigeons.

In the winter, we would sled on the hills behind the house, build forts and tunnels in the deep snow along the lane, and if the lane was snowed in, Deda would meet us at the gate with a bobsled pulled by horses to take us up to the house—what a magical place to visit!

Nothing in the house was modern. There was no electricity, no running water, no indoor plumbing, so it was hard work preparing a meal for the big family. Water had to be carried in a bucket from the well located in the front yard. One hoped there was a breeze so the old windmill would help bring up the water to the pump; otherwise, we had to pump by hand. Water was heated on the wood stove for doing the dishes, and we all drank from the same dipper located by the water bucket at the sink.

Using a toilet meant going to a little shed behind the house, climbing up on a wood bench with a hole in it, holding your nose, and wiping with a page or two from the Montgomery Ward or Sears catalog. If you wrinkled the pages a lot in your hands, they would feel a little softer. Insects, especially spiders and flies, and occasionally a mouse, could often be found in this very special place.

In really bad weather, the kids would climb the narrow staircase to the upstairs and explore the spare bedroom or the attic. The attic was full of wonderful items, especially the really old clothes we could dress up in and put on a fashion show. There was a doll cradle my Deda built for my mom when she was a little girl, which I begged for and was given to take home. That cradle has been handed down to my daughter and now belongs to my granddaughter. There were lots of treasures in that attic, many of which I wish I still had today.

Everyone left the farm in the late afternoon or early in the evening since it was important to get home before dark. Those families that still farmed had to be home to feed the livestock, and those of us living in Cedar Rapids had to set out early enough to allow time for automobile breakdowns. It was always sad to leave, but I looked forward to the next holiday or family celebration.

Sometimes during the summer months Mother would make the trip to the farm driving by herself with my sister and me. On several occasions I was allowed to bring my best friend, Karen, which made for a really fun day. We would ask if we had to bring Aunt Mame along as well. She was my Babi's aunt, quite old, especially to us. She always dressed in black or dreary clothing and she was terribly boring. Mother's answer was always the same, "Yes, of course, that's the only time Babi gets to see her."

So off we would go picking up Aunt Mame on the way, while we three girls giggled in the back seat making fun of Aunt Mame. How I wish I had the opportunity to visit with her now and hear the many stories I am sure she could tell us.

A closer look at the farm house

My Sister Sandra

I was an only child for over five years. Life revolved around me and my many activities.

Sally and her mom when she was the center of attention

One day as I happily bounced into the house for a drink of water after playing outside with some of the neighbor kids, I found my mom curled up on the kitchen floor moaning in pain. I didn't know what was wrong with her, and became so scared I ran to the neighbor across the street for help. Pearl was one of my mom's best friends who came right over, talked to my mom, and then got their car and took me with my mom to the hospital. She called my dad at work and he met us there. Pearl took me to stay with her family. I didn't understand that my mom was in something called labor, but on March 2, 1947, a baby girl joined our family

I insisted she be named Sandra after a special friend I met in school that was older than me but someone I greatly admired, so Sandra or Sandy she was.

Mother with me and three-month-old Sandra

Dad with three month old Sandra

Since there was a difference of a little over five years between our ages, I didn't pay much attention to her in the early days.

But I enjoyed the activity our new baby brought us.

Sandra was born with silver-blonde hair and eyes the color of coal. My mother's Uncle Dirk took one look at her and named her bullets. That's what she was called by the members of my mom's family. We called her Sandy at home.

I don't remember a lot about growing up with my sister. Our personalities were worlds apart. I was studious and more introverted—Sandy was outgoing, not very interested in school, and full of energy.

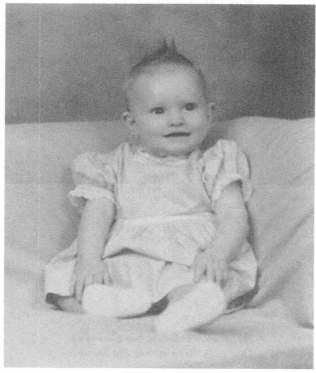

Sister Sandy

Because our house was very small with only two bedrooms, we had to share a room. When Sandy had outgrown her crib, army bunk beds were purchased. When we took them apart and placed them side by side, you had to crawl over one to get to the other—a real problem for keeping them made up. We took turns sleeping in the one next to the window, especially in the summer when you might catch a cool breeze during the night. There was only one closet and it was so small it is hard to imagine fitting all the clothes for two girls into it, but then we didn't have all the different pairs of shoes and outfits children have today.

As Sandy got older, she was just an annoyance, following me around and wanting to do whatever my friends and I were doing. I do remember trying to give her fine straight hair permanent waves to make her hair curly. We tried this on several occasions to no avail. By the morning after, the curls would be gone and the hair would be straight again. To this day, she wears her hair very short and close to the scalp.

We always had pets while we were growing up—at least one dog, a cat or two, and a couple of parakeets. It was always an argument over who was going to clean the bird cage. It was not a sad occasion when they died. The dog and cats were housed outdoors. Spot, the dog, had a beautiful detailed dog house someone built for him. I don't think it was our dad, but perhaps it was, when he was recovering from his accident. We had this dog house for many years and we were very proud of it, putting rags and straw inside to keep Spot warm.

Two and a half year old Sally in front of the dog house

The cats just found a place in the garage or chicken coop in which to sleep or hide. As we grew older, we were often left alone. We had chores assigned to us each day and we knew our boundaries. One day while Mother and Dad were working, Sandy and I decided we should bring one of the cats indoors to play with. After tiring of the petting and playing, we left her to her own devices and forgot about her roaming the house, darting around and behind the furniture. Suddenly, we both smelled something terrible—the cat had done a job under Sandy's bed. We knew we had to clean the mess up before our parents got home or we would be in big trouble. The smell was so strong we tied handkerchiefs over our nose and mouth, found a bucket and rags and proceeded to clean, gagging and choking the entire time. We were just thankful the floor was hard wood and not carpet. We sure learned a lesson. It was the last time we brought the cat indoors.

I have always had a pet or two throughout my life, and loved each one, some more than others. My husband and I have had golden retrievers for the last several years, and we swear our latest one understands English as well as we do. We speak to her in complete sentences as she quietly sits looking at us with her dark brown eyes and blinking her long eyelashes.

There have been reports on the news about various cases of cruelty to animals. How anyone could harm an innocent animal is totally beyond my understanding. I couldn't help but think back to an incident I witnessed as a child. I was probably six or seven years old playing with a little boy in our back yard. His family was new to the neighborhood. I didn't know him very well. I was showing him the baby Bantam chicks my dad so proudly raised, which were happily scratching around in the chicken yard. For some unknown reason, this little boy picked up a garden hoe leaning against one of the chicken coops and proceeded to chop the head off one of the baby chicks. I stood by watching in horror. I ran into the house crying and telling my mother what happened. She immediately went outside and sent the little boy home. He was not allowed to play at our house ever again. Even after all these years, I remember the incident vividly. I often wonder what happened to that boy as he grew up, and if his streak of cruelty carried forward into adulthood.

Another memorable occasion was a night our parents were out with friends. Sandy and I were in the living room when there was a knock on the windows by the front porch door. We ignored it at first and then the knock was harder and louder until the glass broke and pieces fell into the house along with my mother's African violets which she kept on shelves in the window.

Opening the front door, three boys from my grade at school were standing there with guilty looks on their faces. We were in the seventh grade and boys and girls were just beginning to be aware of each other, so often traveled to each other's houses. After much apologizing by the boys, I sent them on their way. Sandy and I had another mess to clean up. An explanation to our parents was accepted. The broken window was later repaired, since weather was not a factor.

As I was recently having lunch with my sister, I asked her what she remembered about us growing up. She couldn't remember much, she said, since I was not often around. The difference in our ages accounted for that since I started working away from home at the age of eleven, and would have been gone a lot from that time on. She did remember chasing me outside our house and around the yard, knocking me down and beating on me for taking a piece of her red licorice from her bag of candy. It wasn't funny at the time, but we can laugh about it now.

As we grew older, married and had children, we became much closer. Losing our parents at a fairly early age made a difference as well, and now she is one of my best friends. She is divorced and both of her daughters, with their families, live out of state, so we feel free to call upon each other for special needs. We both love to shop and travel. We often try different places for lunch. We share holidays and special occasions. My sister is no longer an annoyance but a blessing.

Sandy's happy second birthday

Sandy and Sally, check out the hair styles

Sandy and Sally as adults 2019

GROWING UP

My childhood was not unlike other kids my age and if it was, I didn't know it. I had many friends cultivated from the neighborhood, from school, church and later the jobs I held. With both parents working, certain chores were expected to be done and free time was available to pursue hobbies and my personal interests. We had our own fears but without social media and up to the minute news coverage, they were not as dramatic due to limited exposure. I have written about many of these encounters in the pages following.

Childhood Friends

During World War II, there were shortages of tires, gasoline, sugar, and other commodities which could only be purchased using ration coupons. Neighbors were close during that time, and deep friendships were formed. I became friends with a little boy next door named Terry, and two girls, Janet and Carol, from across the road. I call it a road because our house was on the edge of town and the streets were gravel. Over the winter, the snowplows pushed the gravel aside. After the spring thaw, the streets became full of deep muddy ruts from the cars trying to get through. We would have to leave our car on the closest hard-surface road, and walk to our house. After the muddy road dried out, the grader would come through to level the ruts and add gravel.

My mother was very proud of her little girl with long blond curls. When I was about two-and-a-half years old she bought me a pretty new dress and fancy bonnet to wear to the family Easter celebration on the farm.

One day Dad was supposed to be taking care of me while Mother was at work. Janet came over. We decided to "play barber" in the corner of the living room. Guess who got their hair cut—no more long blond curls under that fancy bonnet. My mother cried and cried when she got a look at me upon coming home from work.

Janet was a little older than I, and Carol was a little younger. We played together almost every day. Their father worked at Quaker Oats and was of German descent and very strict. He would often bring home treasures from work, including empty patterned flour sacks, which he shared with my mother and me. I couldn't wait to make pretty circular skirts out of them, which was all the rage in the 1950s. My mother made fancy aprons and other practical things for the house. I thought these neighbors were very rich because the girls played the piano and took dance lessons. Their mother made them beautiful costumes from fancy tulle, beads, and sequins for their dance recitals. I was so jealous of them, but I learned one day that if they misbehaved, their father had a terrible temper, and would beat them with his leather belt. When I saw the bleeding welts on Janet's back one day, I decided being poor wasn't so bad after all.

My friend, Terry, and I would explore in the field next to the house. Sometimes we would walk to the railroad tracks to place pennies on the track before a train came so they would be flattened. We would often find mice in the field which we would catch, put them in a big rain barrel, and watch then run in circles trying to get out. In the winter, we would walk to the creek hoping it was covered in ice for another adventure, skating, sliding, and sometimes falling through.

Terry lived with his mom and younger brother in a little house next to his grandmother's. We had an apple orchard between the properties so you could often find us climbing in the apple trees.

My friend Terry and I on his trike

37

Another friend, Karen, moved into the neighborhood after we were in town school. We became very good friends, spending many a night together with sleepovers, mostly at her house, because of my father's drinking. She was an only child at that time, and her parents always made me feel welcome. We were often dreaming up schemes to make spending money, and our favorite was weaving pot holders. We wove them in a variety of colors using a loom and special fabric loops. We sold them to family members and some of the neighborhood moms. Sometimes Terry joined us and we would get dressed up in old clothes and put on a play.

Sandy, me, Karen, Terry

Karen's dad was a great fisherman and each year her family took a vacation to Leech Lake in Minnesota. I was invited along for many of those vacations. I learned how to fish and loved it. How exciting it was to feel that tug on the end of the line and the pull on the pole towards the water. We caught walleyes, northern pike, and perch. Nothing was better tasting than fried fish fresh from the lake. When we weren't fishing, we explored the woods around the cabin. Sometimes we took day trips to the head of the Mississippi

River in Itasca State Park, or the iron mine fields in northern Minnesota. Sometimes Karen's parents would drive us to the dump at night to watch the bears forage for food. Those vacations were magical for me, and gave me an opportunity to broaden my scope of experiences beyond our home. Karen and I remained friends for many years acting as maid of honor at each other's wedding.

Without television and electronics, friends were my greatest source of entertainment. I remember one young boy who used to come by on his horse and take me for horseback rides. A group of us used to ride bicycles together. Sometimes we stopped to buy honey from a friend's grandmother who raised bees.

A memory as a child related to a particularly hot summer day. Prohibition was long over, but people continued to make their own alcohol, usually beer or wine. Our neighbor had quite a sophisticated wine-making system in his basement, but being of German descent, that was not unusual. Our father brewed beer in order to cut costs for his drinking. When he came home from work carrying the paper bag with cans of malt extract, my little sister, five years younger, and I would look at each other and silently mouth the words, "Oh, No!" We knew another batch of home brew would be in the making.

The beer fermented in a huge open crock in the basement fruit cellar. The fruit cellar was an area dug off the basement, with dirt walls and floor. That is where canned goods, potatoes, onions, and other food items were stored. After mixing up the ingredients for the beer, they were added to the open crock and left to work for seven to ten days. When the beer was "ready," I was required to help with the bottling.

This process involved the hated task of washing the bottles, scrubbing each one with a bottle brush in soapy water, and carefully rinsing them. Filling the bottles with beer was the fun part, making sure the siphon tube was kept off the bottom of the crock so the sediment was not disturbed. The caps were then applied with a special capper tool attached to a pine board placed between your legs. Each bottle was lined up under the capper and the caps had to be put on just right so the beer wouldn't spoil—like there was ever enough time for that to happen before it was all gone. Then my father would make another batch.

Most beer was made in five-gallon batches, but I remember a huge crock sitting on a wooden pedestal. Each batch required lots of bottles to prepare, fill, and cap. This also meant our father was drinking nightly instead of just on weekends. He would often fill a fruit jar—a clear glass quart canning jar—as a "tasting" glass prior to the beer being ready for bottling. This was toxic stuff and quickly went to his head.

During one of the brewing batches, a girl friend and I were playing outdoors. My little sister was tagging along as usual, when we decided we were bored and should check out the crock of beer. We thought a little taste would be refreshing since it was very hot outdoors, so down to the fruit cellar we went. The plastic tubing was coiled on top of the crock, but standing on my tip toes, I could reach it, and knew just how to get a syphon started. You just sucked on one end of the tube with the other end in the liquid until the beer started to run out. We took turns drinking from the syphon hose until we had our fill and went back outdoors to continue playing.

When my parents got home from work, my father went into the basement to find his beer running all over the floor and down the drain. We had left the syphon hose hanging over the side of the crock, which continued to drain the beer. There was much yelling and cursing. I was left with a loud scolding and warning to stay away from the brew in the future, although that didn't eliminate my chore of having to

40

help my father bottle his beer. After assuring my father it would never happen again, I tearfully went to our bedroom feeling ashamed and experiencing a belly full of beer farts.

In the early years of growing up, my best friends, were from the neighborhood. We all went to the same one-room school and we all lived within walking distance of one another. One friend was a couple of years older than I, and she and her younger sister lived just across the road from us. As we grew a little older, probably nine or ten, our boundaries began to expand beyond the immediate neighborhood. Janet, my older friend, was allowed to go to the movies downtown without parental supervision. One Saturday she invited me to go along. Janet was so much more experienced in the ways of the world. She gave me my first haircut when I was little.

I was so excited to be allowed to go with her, and was given a small allowance to do some shopping at McLellan's dime store, pay for my movie ticket and even get a treat at Woolworth's soda counter, another downtown dime store. Her mother gave us a ride to the theatre, and told us what time and where she would pick us up. Wow, we were on our own—quite an adventure for me. Feeling all grown up, into the movie we went.

After the movie was over, we walked from the Paramount Theatre to McLellan's dime store to shop. Decals were all the rage at that time—you could put them on lots of things and use them for all kinds of decorating. Remember, I had limited funds to spend so Janet explained we could buy one or two decals, which would give us a sack—then when no one was looking, we could slip some more into the sack without paying for them. I didn't think this was a good idea, but she convinced me no one would know, and we would have all the decals we wanted. Okay, I said, and we proceeded with our plan. I thought it was a bit risky, but the plan worked, and we left the store to wait for our ride home.

41

Upon arriving at home, I proudly showed my mother all the decals I had acquired and explained how I was able to get so many. She was horrified with what I had done and told me I was a thief and could go to jail for stealing. She promptly put me in the car to take me back to the dime store to pay for the decals or return them and fess up to my crime with the store clerks. I was terrified walking into the store but knew I had to clear my name. Shaking in my boots, I walked up to the counter where the decals were being displayed and when no one was looking I sneaked them from my sack back onto the counter. As I completed the task I set out to do, I felt a big sigh of relief at not being caught and sent to jail. I quickly left the store and joined my mother waiting in the car to return home. We didn't talk about it anymore and I didn't have the heart to tell her exactly how I solved the problem, but I certainly learned an unforgettable lesson about honesty.

Summer Vacation Visiting the Farm

During the time I was in grade school, summer vacation usually meant a trip to my grandparent's farm for a get together with most of the cousins and my aunts and uncles on a Sunday, and then I would be left for a stay of one week or more. I looked forward to this since if I stayed long enough, it usually meant my grandparents taking me with them to the Amanas to buy groceries at the General Store. If I was lucky, Babi would buy me a box of old fashion ginger snap cookies. My mouth would water just thinking about this wonderful treat dipped in a glass of milk fresh from the cow. Store bought cookies were a rarity and a real luxury.

A visit to the Amana General Store for supplies was a treat in itself. That store had everything from soup to nuts. Sometimes we would stop in the woolen mill or the furniture shop to just look around. I don't remember Babi and Deda ever buying anything, I think they just wanted to visit with the locals. We also made a stop at the meat market with its wonderful aroma of smoked meats. A ham to roast or a few slices of schwartenmagen also known as head cheese to be eaten on rye bread was a real delicacy. As a matter of definition, head cheese is made from pig heads. There is no cheese in it, so I'm not sure why it's called head cheese, but there is a lot of tasty meat in the head of the hog. My husband and I still make visits to the Amana smoke house and meat shop for this tasty meat similar to a chunky pate, best eaten on fresh rye bread or with crackers.

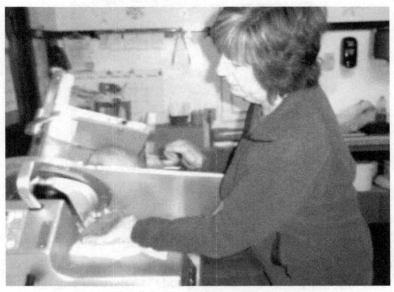

Amana Butcher Shop: Slicing the head cheese

Ready to eat slice of head cheese

Jaternice: a special blend of pork products in a casing

After reminiscing over certain foods we grew up eating as children, we recently made a road trip to Polasheks Locker in Protivin, Iowa, Protivin is an early Czech community settled in the early 1900's and is home to a meat locker retailing many of the "bizarre" foods we used to eat and are still available.

Many years ago my husband was waiting by my office to take me home after work when a co-worker leaned in the car window to chat with him. My husband wondered why he kept glancing into the back seat forgetting his mother had given him two of the jaternice in a plastic bag to take home for dinner. We laughed and laughed when we realized what our friend saw and what he must have been thinking.

Babi and Deda did butcher on the farm, mostly a hog, but without refrigeration, the meat was usually canned in quart jars. Their adult children would share in the meat provided. Babi and Deda lived very simply. The farm house did not have electricity so when the sun set, kerosene lamps were lit to provide light until bedtime which came fairly early. The motto was, "early to bed, early to rise." Early to rise meant doing morning chores which consisted of feeding the chickens, making sure they had water and picking their eggs. The cows would be in their stalls of the barn and needed to be milked. Deda would feed the pigs and the extra milk separated from the cream would be dumped into the hog trough since they did not get enough milk to make it worth selling.

After milking the cows, the raw milk was taken to an old stone building called the milk house. There was a large water reservoir built into one end with a wide shuttered opening towards the barnyard where the cows, or if there were horses, could come up to, stick their heads in and drink the water. I remember the walls around the water were covered with moss and the bottom of the tank was a yucky looking green slime but there was always a supply of water so it must have been spring fed. I think if you looked closely, there were also some catfish swimming lazily along the bottom.

The milk house building was always cool and the other half of it housed the separator. The raw milk was poured into a bowl and by turning a crank, the milk was separated from the cream. The cream came out of one tube and the skim milk out of the other. The cream was used to make butter for special occasions or used in baking

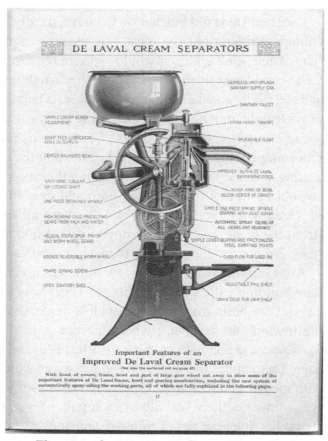

The parts of a separator similar to the one used

This is what the butter churn resembled

I didn't like the chickens and was afraid of the cows, so I just tagged along to watch Babi work. It was fascinating to see the separator work as well as the churning of butter. The farm cats seemed to know when this process would take place and always showed up in time for Babi to pour some of the fresh milk into an old saucer kept on the floor just for them. Churning butter was something I could help with until the butter got too thick for me to turn the paddles. The type of butter churn Babi used was glass similar to the picture shown. We did this in the kitchen and churning butter usually meant company was coming soon since butter could only be kept a short time without pasteurization and refrigeration, but oh my, was it good when freshly made and lathered on warm baked biscuits.

Let me digress a moment back to the time we started to use substitute butter at home. We referred to it as oleo and it came in a small sealed plastic bag with a capsule of dye located within the bag. Since the oleo or now referred to as margarine was naturally white in color at that time, the capsule was broken in the bag and the bag kneaded until the dye was distributed throughout the package giving it a color more like butter instead of lard. I always begged my mom to let me do the squeezing since I felt like I was doing magic turning that artificial butter from white to a creamy yellow.

When the morning chores were finished on the farm, breakfast was eaten, the dishes cleaned up and it was time to head to the garden. We would hoe or weed and pick those vegetables that were ready for use in a meal. One summer while visiting was strawberry season. I really loved strawberries and ate so many I broke out in hives all over my body. We never did really know if the hives were caused by the strawberries since I had a lot of allergies in my youth, but they appeared to be the immediate culprit. My mother was called to come and get me since I was miserable and couldn't stand the itching. A few days at home and several applications of calamine lotion calmed the itching and the hives disappeared.

Using the telephone to call someone was an art in itself. The old telephone hung on the wall and had a crank with a ringer. It was a party line and anybody using it heard all of the neighbors' calls by the rings they made. Two longs and one short meant a certain neighbor and Babi would pick up the receiver to listen in if she felt so inclined to hear the latest gossip. Calling my mom from the farm to Cedar Rapids meant going through an operator. We had a party line at home, but our phones were considered modern with numbers to dial to reach the person you were calling. A few people had a private line, but most of my parent's friends or families in the city had a two, three or four party line. If you had an emergency, it was okay to interrupt, otherwise you waited until the line was clear to make your call.

Taking a bath on the farm was an interesting experience since there was no running water and definitely not a bathroom so you didn't bathe very often. If you were going somewhere special or if it had been several days, we would drag out a round galvanized steel tub into the middle of the kitchen, fill it with cold water from the well in a bucket and warm the water with hot water heated on the wood burning stove. In the summer, water would be taken from the well and left out in the sun to warm up. If memory serves me, I think we had Ivory bar soap for bathing or a bar soap purchased from the Watkins man or maybe even homemade soap, but certainly not the lovely smelling soaps and lotions available today. You quickly scrubbed yourself and couldn't wait to dry off using the stiff scratchy towels that had been hung outside on the clothesline to dry. When I stayed at my cousin's farm, they had indoor plumbing and a real bathtub, but you still didn't waste water by bathing too often.

My cousin's farm was located close to Fairfax. There were three girls and one boy and they lived on a very active grain and livestock farm. My visits there were never very long because the older children had to work hard helping out. Donna Jean was the oldest girl and closest to my age. Donnie was the oldest and only boy so they were required to do most of the chores while the two younger girls were allowed to play. My uncle would work in the fields and my aunt did all the cooking, baking, housework and laundry. There was always a big garden to care for and then fall canning of the produce for use over winter.

My fondest memory related to Donna Jean's pet cow named Bossy. We would go out into the field to collect her and then I would get to ride her back into the barn yard. What a treat that was for me to ride on Bossy's bony old back as she ambled slowly along a well-worn path with a cow bell ringing from around her neck. I wasn't afraid of Bossy because she was so gentle, and since she was too old to milk, she just hung out with other cows. I don't remember what ultimately happened to her, but knowing my uncle, if you didn't produce income in one way or another, you were gone, another reason for not visiting too long.

I was always a little afraid of my Uncle Edwin. He had a stern look, was rather loud and not the gentle type of person like my Aunt Wilma. They were married for over 75 years so I determined he wasn't mean or scary when as an adult I got to know him better and realized they had a real love relationship going on. Although my uncle died in his 90's, my mom's sister, Wilma, lived until her 100th birthday before passing on. Each summer, a visit to the farm was different, and each visit created a special memory.

Family Vacations

A family vacation usually meant going to a cabin owned by friends of my parents for a week. The cabin was located on the Wapsi River near a small town called Waubeek, and was a great spot for relaxing, fishing, and playing in the river. The cabin was not very large, consisting of a kitchen, living room, and one bedroom. The toilet was an outhouse in the backyard behind the shed used to hold the boat and equipment for yard maintenance and fishing.

The cabin facing the river

We often had the son of my mother's best friend with us. His father was in the navy, and his mother would visit his dad whenever he was stationed close by. The son's name was Melvin, but we called him Mickey all his life. He was close to my age, nine or ten, and like a brother. We slept in the living room which had multiple couches used for beds. I remember one night being cool and covered with a blanket that turned out to be wool. In the middle of the night I woke up gasping for air and unable to breathe. Who knew I had asthma and was allergic to wool. I certainly avoided wool in the future, including a wool coat which gave my arms a bad case of eczema. I finally grew out of these allergies when I became pregnant, and passed them on to my children and ultimately my grandchildren.

Using a log as a teeter totter over the river

The cabin's backyard had horseshoe pits set up for entertainment and friendly competition. The front yard was large, leading to the river bank and dock for tying up the boat, fishing, or sun bathing. Certain parts of the river were quite shallow and were great for wading or swimming. One day while playing in the river with Mickey and my little

51

sister, I stepped on a piece of broken glass and cut my big toe quite deeply. As I think back now, it would have required several stitches and a tetanus shot, but back then my mom just used some iodine as an antiseptic, and then bandaged it with gauze and tape. I was not able to go back into the river until it healed, so I limped around for several days, still being barefooted.

One of the favorite things for Mickey and me to do was try catching carp by spearing them in the backwaters with a special tool. We were never successful, but it was fun trying.

If the weather was not good, or in the evenings after we gave up fishing and playing outdoors, our entertainment consisted of board games, playing cards, working jigsaw puzzles, or reading. There were no electronics or even a television. An old radio with poor reception was available, but the stations were limited and not very interesting.

We would stay a week, from Saturday until the following Sunday. The owners, known as Porky and Jessie, would show up with several other friends for a huge picnic with lots of beer, pop, and good food. Hot dogs and hamburgers with potato chips were a special treat. There was ample beer drinking, horseshoe playing, and storytelling. Sunday evening came much too quickly, and it was time to pack up, clean the cabin and grounds, and head for home dreaming of the next cabin vacation.

Camping and Fishing

Proudly posing with her catch of the day. Sally, Dad, & Sandy

Fishing was something my dad enjoyed doing, and we could do it as a family with a minimum of expense. His dream was to buy a fishing boat when he retired. In the meantime, we fished from river banks. We had inexpensive fishing poles, some bamboo with or without reels, and some more modern ones. If there was a long weekend, we would pack up food, drinks, clothing, fishing equipment, blankets, and an old canvas tarp we used for a makeshift tent. We would head to the Ivanhoe Bridge which crossed the Cedar River southeast of Cedar Rapids. We set up our camp site, usually with another couple and their son who was a good friend and close to my age. We spent the weekend fishing. This was where I learned to fish as a small child. I didn't usually catch anything except underground tree limbs, garbage, and once in a while a softshell turtle which reminded me of a snake. They would always swallow the hook so we had to cut the line to free them. When not fishing, we would play on a sandy beach along the water's edge. The river was too treacherous for swimming due to fast-moving currents and whirlpools.

Dad napping after several beverages

Prior to going fishing, I would help my dad dig in the garden for fish worms, which were much smaller than the night crawlers people use today. We prepared dough balls or bought stink bait. The dough balls were made from stale bread mixed with water, corn flour, and flavored with anise extract. Stink bait was usually purchased in a jar, and was very smelly. Sometimes my dad would pick up fresh chicken livers or innards at a butcher shop on 16th Avenue in Czech

Village to use as bait. Both were applied to a treble hook which held the bait on better, and was tied to the fishing line, along with a lead sinker, to keep the line low in the water. The smellier the bait, the better the catfish liked it. If the catfish weren't biting, we would try our luck for carp using canned corn kernels.

Carp were not the fish of choice because of the amount of bones they had. Once they were cleaned and fried with a crispy crust, they were very tasty if you carefully ate around the bones. Fishing for carp was like a sport, hoping you caught the biggest one.

A favorite place to fish for carp was under the railroad bridge by Quaker Oats, using canned corn for bait. The spilled grain was a great feeding ground for fish as well as rats. It was a challenge to keep them away.

Once I began traveling with my friend's family to Minnesota, her dad taught me a different kind of fishing in the lakes. We used minnows (tiny fish) for bait and were usually hoping to catch walleyes, a very tasty fish. We would also catch sunfish, bluegills, and after dark on a smaller lake, we would fish for bullheads, a smaller version of a catfish. These were wonderful vacations for me since we would visit some of the tourist attractions in northern Minnesota if the fish weren't biting. After dark we would drive to the local dump to watch the bears forage for food. We found this exciting as we sat in the car—with the windows rolled up.

After marriage, my husband and I would annually travel to Canada with another couple to a rustic cabin in the woods on a remote lake. We would stay a week and fish for walleye, northern pike, and bass. We mostly used minnows or artificial lures. We each had our favorite lure, mine being a silver spoon shape which spun in the water as the boat slowly moved around the lake. This was called trolling. Getting a hit always made my heart race until the fish was actually hooked and brought in, so we could identify it and determine if it was a keeper. Some of the keepers would be cleaned and cooked for shore lunch—nothing better than fresh fried fish with a cold beer from the ever-present cooler.

Although we no longer do much fishing, I have many pleasant memories of this wonderful activity with friends—impossible to forget.

Sally with Canadian friends enjoying a shore lunch

... and trolling on the lake

Entertainment Growing Up

When my father was drinking, I spent most evenings with my mother doing things we both enjoyed. In the winter we worked jigsaw puzzles, laying out all the pieces on a card table that we could stash in a corner of the room until it was completed. We would enjoy the picture for a few days after completing it, and then take it all apart and put it back in the box. The puzzles were then traded with a neighbor for a new picture. This hobby must have been a carryover from my mom's dad. Grandpa had a huge puzzle picture framed and hung in the kitchen over a couch located in a corner. As a child I thought it must have had thousands of pieces since it was so large. I remember looking at this picture so often because a piece of the puzzle had fallen out of place and was lying along the bottom of the frame inside the glass. This really bothered me, and I often wonder whatever happened to that picture when Grandma and Grandpa moved off the farm.

Playing cards was another favorite pastime. My mom and dad belonged to a card club which met once a month. The members took turns hosting it and the kids were taken along to play their own card or board games. When we kids got tired in the winter we curled up on a bed amongst everybody's coats. In the summer we slept on a sofa, the back porch swing, or in a hammock. We played a lot of board games at home as well. The favorites were Monopoly, Clue, Chinese Checkers, or just regular checkers. Another favorite card game was Authors. I can still remember some of the classic books that were on the cards.

As I grew older, I learned to play most of the card games adults played, and many a winter weekend was spent playing pinochle with my mom, my friend Janet, and her

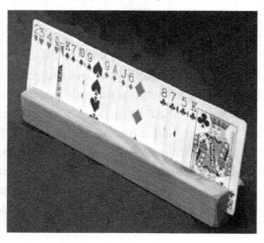

mom. We played four-handed double-deck pinochle, which meant too many cards in your hand. So Janet's dad, able to build most anything, built us card holders so we could arrange our cards in a line and easily see which ones we wanted to play. I thought they were made out of wood similar to the one pictured, but recently learned ours were metal. There was a lot of laughing and enjoyment at these gatherings which always included special snacks and age-appropriate beverages.

Certain nights, especially Sundays, were spent listening to the radio. Our favorite programs were Jack Benny and Amos 'n' Andy. After dinner, we eagerly cleaned up the kitchen so we could gather around the old living room radio and listen to these shows. The radio was a table-top radio similar to the one shown. The sound wasn't the greatest, but we enjoyed the shows being broadcast anyway.

A form of outdoor entertainment was roller skating. My memory is of a metal plate with four wheels and four adjustable clamps that attached to your shoes. I seem to remember a special key used to tighten or loosen the clamps. I would skate back and forth and up and down the concrete sidewalks in our back yard until my legs would be too tired to move. Skating was so popular. Roller rinks were built where you could rent skates, which were lace-up boots with polyurethane wheels attached, and designed for more fancy footwork on the polished floor. Music would be playing, and singles or couples would perform dance moves on their skates under a crystal ball hanging from the ceiling. There were colored lights sparkling off the mosaic tiles. I never got good enough to dance or even skate backward, since the cost prohibited me from going to the rink very often. But I could get out on the floor away from the hand railing.

In the 1950s, drive-in theaters were built in Cedar Rapids and became a source of after-dark entertainment for families. Teenagers would drive with their dates and groups of friends. A drive-in consisted of a large outdoor movie screen, a projection booth in the middle of the parking lot along with a concession stand. Cars would park next to posts with individual speakers connected by a wire. We would hang the speakers on our car window. We could control the volume with a knob on the speaker. We would take our own snacks and a cooler full of iced beverages, and off to the movies we would go. If admission was charged per person, some kids would hide in the trunk or under a blanket in the back seat to save money.

Once television became part of in-home entertainment, declining attendance in drive-ins became common and they were no longer profitable. In climates such as Iowa, they also could only be used on a seasonal basis. That discouraged them as an investment so they slowly closed one after another.

One day our favorite neighbor announced they were getting a television. This was so exciting I could hardly wait until we were invited over to watch special programs on a little oblong screen in their living room. Once installed, we were invited to come over to see this phenomenon. Sometimes the screen was so snowy it was difficult to see the images, but we were impressed with this amazing piece of entertainment. It became a regular invitation to watch Liberace play the piano, and World Wide Wrestling—everybody's favorite shows. We each had our favorite wrestler we faithfully followed.

As time went on, television watching became more commonplace as technology improved. Antennas were capturing better signals and more stations were coming on the air. Prices began to be more affordable. One day my mom took my sister and me to the appliance store to buy our very own TV. It was a beautiful wood console with a huge black and white screen (probably 19 inch) and we couldn't wait to get it home. By that time, rabbit ears—an indoor antenna that sat on top of your television set—were in use so a rooftop antenna was no longer necessary. If the signal was not strong, we hung strips of tin foil from the arms of the rabbit ears to help improve the reception. We were in seventh heaven having our very own television to watch. Now Sunday nights shifted from the radio to the TV with our favorite program being the Ed Sullivan Show. I guess the invention of television was the beginning of the inactivity of children, and some adults, today.

An early television set and rabbit ears

Chores

When both parents were working, my sister and I were expected to perform certain chores. We were responsible for keeping our room clean, making sure the house was tidy, and performing kitchen duty. We did not have to do any cooking, so my sister never did learn how, and to this day has no interest. So her stove is always spotless. We did have to clear the table after meals, and of course, doing dishes was always part of kitchen duty. We had a little step stool to stand on at the kitchen sink, and we took turns washing and drying the dishes, and putting them away. Since my sister was six years younger, she always got the easiest of the designated chores.

Our biggest chore was helping with laundry. Wash day was a big event. The wringer washer would be pulled out so the garden-type hose from the hot water spigot could reach to fill it. Then the double rinse tubs would be pulled alongside the washer and filled with cold water. The clothes would be sorted into three piles. One was my dad's work clothes which included bib overalls. The whites included sheets. The third was colored clothes. The whites would be washed first. They were placed into the washer with its agitator, and washed for several minutes. Then the wooden washing stick, which was like a modified broom handle, would be used to pick up the hot clothes and run them through a wringer positioned over a rinse tub. The wringer was a double roller on a swivel so its position could be changed from washer to rinse tub, and from rinse tub to the second rinse tub, and finally into the clothes basket for taking outdoors to hang.

As kids, we thought helping with the wash was a fun chore—it must have been because playing in water was always enjoyable. My sister tells the story of running clothes through the wringer and getting her hand caught and pulled in with the clothes. Instead of hitting the release button which opened the rollers, our mother panicked and set the

wringer to reverse and rolled her hand back out. Of course it hurt, but the wash continued. This was usually an all-day process and reminded us why we didn't change clothes until they were really dirty.

Once the clothes were taken outside to dry, they were hung on lines in the back yard or the side yard. Clothes lines were strung between metal posts which were great for playing on when not in use. They were our version of monkey bars.

There was a set procedure on how the clothes were hung. If the weather was raining, or such that it was impossible to dry outdoors, a couple of lines were strung in the basement. We also set up wooden tripods for drying smaller items. Drying indoors was not the best option since you did not get that fresh-air smell.

Once the clothes were dry, we were sent out to "pick them." That meant removing the clothes pins and placing them in a hanging bag, folding the clothes in a manner with the least amount of wrinkling, and putting them back into the clothes basket. If some items needed ironing, they were placed into a special basket. You can see how this was an all-day job.

Sally on her backyard monkey bars

Another big chore was working in the garden. We had two large gardens, one planted with sweet corn and the other with a variety of vegetables. Everything was done by hand or hand tools. Each hole for the sweet corn was dug in a row, with a certain number of seeds placed in each, and then covered with dirt. A string was streched across the field so the rows would be straight, and then moved the appropriate space for the next row.

The other garden was used for potatoes, onions, beans, peas, radishes, carrots, cabbage, cucumbers, and lettuce. These were the most basic vegetables which could be kept in the fruit cellar for winter, or processed and canned. Each type of vegetable had its own seed and procedure for planting in the rows, which were marked as to type by empty seed packages that were placed on sticks at the end of each row. As the seeds developed and began pushing through the soil, the garden would have to be kept free from weeds, which meant using a hoe or iron rake to work up the soil. This was back-breaking hard work, but having fresh vegetables for dinner was a special treat. We especially liked the lettuce when it was creamed. Radishes were always enjoyed, especially when my sister and I had burping contests afterward. Cucumbers were eaten as a salad or pickled in crocks. Cabbage, corn, and tomatoes usually meant a dedicated day of canning whenever they were ready.

Excess cabbage was made into sauerkraut, another all-day chore. Glass jars were brought out of storage and sterilized by washing in hot soapy water and then boiled to kill any bacteria. Lids were usually purchased new, although in the early days lids of zinc with white porcelain tops were reused over and over. The heads of cabbage were cut, the outer leaves removed, and the heads cut in half to place in the cutter box to be moved back and forth over the cutting blades. The shredded cabbage was packed into the clean jars with salt and a hot brine pored over the top. Lids were loosely placed on the jars until it was determined the cabbage had turned into sauerkraut. The jars were then stored on shelving in the fruit room. Canning corn was a similar endeavor. The husks, and as much of the silk as possible, had to be removed from the ears of corn. Then a sharp knife was used to cut the kernels off the cob. The corn was then processed according to the current canning procedures. This procedure was also followed for green beans as well as tomatoes. Tomatoes could be canned whole, as juice, sauce, or even ketchup.

The peas rarely made it out of the garden, since as soon as the pods were beginning to fill out, we would crawl along the rows, eating them right in the garden. We also had apple trees, raspberry and blackberry bushes, and plum trees to harvest. Some of the fruit was eaten fresh, and the rest preserved.

The other summer-time chore was mowing and trimming the grass. This was all done with a push lawn mower and hand clippers. We lived on a rather large lot; there was plenty of grass to mow and places to trim around.

Fall meant potatoes were dug and stored in bushel baskets in the basement fruit room, onions were dug up, tied in bunches, and hung there as well to dry. Fall was also a time to go foraging for mushrooms with my mother and usually her best friend, Annie. We only hunted fall mushrooms because they were the best for canning. My mother and her friends knew which mushrooms were edible and we looked for only certain ones. A variety often found was known as koza brada or goatsbeards although the button mushroom was the favored variety and created the most excitement when found in large patches. The equipment required for mushroom hunting consisted of a bucket, basket or paper bag, and a knife. We often used a pillow case, dreaming of large finds. A favorite place to forage was known as Averill's Timber, a large tract of land including a bluff overlooking the Cedar River southwest of Cedar Rapids. We could drive into a grassy path, park the car, grab our tools, and head out into the wooded grounds hoping to experience a find.

I often found goatsbeards, but they were usually too old or full of worms. Finding button specimens was the ultimate, especially if they were fleshy, not dried out or decaying. Mushroom hunting was somewhat like fishing—some days you just came up empty. When you had a find, you couldn't wait to holler out and start cutting the mushrooms with your knife, always leaving a portion of the root where it was growing, for future development. If your find was large enough, you could just sit back and enjoy the sights and smells of the timber until the rest of the hunters were ready to leave.

Once home, the mushrooms were dumped onto the kitchen table, where they were sorted and cleaned. Cleaning did not require water, only a brush or a knife to scrape the dirt. They were then used for cooking, or prepared for canning. They were placed into small jars, to be added to various recipes over the winter, especially chili being a favorite. Most mushroom hunters today forage for the spring mushrooms, but to me, there was nothing better than the odor, flavor, and texture of the fall mushrooms, which most closely resembles those sold in the grocery stores.

With all these chores, one wonders how we found time to play and be with friends, but we did, and it is probably why we rarely found time to get into trouble, and why we stayed healthy and physically fit.

Hobbies

My mother quilted by hand but her favorite handwork was tatting. She would sit and tat for hours, especially when she became ill and mobility was a factor. The little rings and knots fascinated me so she tried to teach me. I found it to be a frustrating task, but was determined to learn. I sat in my bedroom, gritting my teeth, and tried and tried to make that shuttle work, tearing knot after knot out of the thread when they wouldn't slide, until finally I mastered it. I was so pleased with myself I couldn't quit making lace trims, doilies, and other trims for pillow cases, and especially handkerchiefs. Kleenex tissues were an unknown when I was growing up, so pretty handkerchiefs were carried. Although I no longer tat, I still remember how. I have my mom's favorite ivory shuttle should I want to take it up and try again someday.

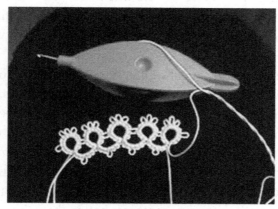

Shuttle for tatting

Mother didn't do much sewing although we had a sewing machine tucked into a corner of the kitchen. It was an old Singer treadle machine. I learned to sew at school in a home economics class. They only taught us how to make an apron, and I wanted to make my own clothes. We didn't have a lot of money to spend on the trendy clothes other kids were wearing. My dear Aunt Helen took me under her wing, and over the summer I would spend a day every now and then at her house learning to sew. Aunt Helen was the wife of one of my mom's brothers and was an expert seamstress. She was an expert at a lot of things since they did not have any children. I would choose a pattern, select the fabric and notions needed, and take them to her house to sew. Her sewing machine was electric and very modern. She taught me how to make belts, cover buckles to match, and all the fine details of finishing an outfit. I learned a lot from Aunt Helen who knew lots of tricks and how to do things to give that professional or store-bought look as well as performing a task to perfection.

An old treadle sewing machine

Sewing has been a long time hobby of mine. I continued to make a lot of my own clothes into my adult life and then for my children until they reached an age that only store-bought would do. I made my son several pairs of brightly colored shorts with coordinating tee shirts when loud pants were all the rage. I still have my old portable Singer sewing machine which we purchased when I was first married. It continues to work just as it did when it was new. Of course it doesn't have any of the bells and whistles with fancy stitches of the newer machines. When I was doing a lot of upholstery work, it was a real work-horse, sewing through many layers and types of fabric.

My wonderful Aunt Helen not only taught me to sew, but tried to teach me to knit as well. After several attempts with stitches so tight we couldn't get them off the needles, she gave up and said I would never be a knitter because I was too tense.

Aunt Helen and Uncle Walter during an anniversary celebration

Late in my adult life, I decided I wanted to give knitting a try again, so I took a class at a knit shop in Marion. The instructor was wonderful and I became a proficient knitter. She was not only a great instructor, but became a friend since we had many of the same interests. I continue to knit regularly and have a stash of yarn that I cannot possibly live long enough to get through. Knitters cannot help but acquire beautiful yarns in colors and textures that your hands just itch to touch.

Uncle Walter's hobby was woodworking. My grandfather clock and curio cabinet were made by him. There was very little he could not make out of wood, including building his own home.

When we lived on the acreage, we had a special building built that served as storage for all the paraphernalia one needs to maintain ten acres of lawn, forest, and a swimming pool. It also became the perfect shop for refinishing furniture. It had a loft overlooking the countryside which became another area to hold another stash, only this stash was unfinished furniture, fine pieces of wood, and supplies for caning and replacing webbing.

One of my best friends and I would scour garage sales and flea markets for interesting pieces of furniture or decorating items. I would strip the paint or varnish off the wood, sand and stain, and apply a final finish to make the piece look like new. I especially loved interesting old chairs. My daughter and I still have a collection of mismatched pieces in beautiful oak or other lovely wood. When we sold the property and moved to the city, the stash moved with us, but I lost interest in this hobby since the new home no longer had the convenient space to work, and the unfinished pieces were ultimately sold in a garage sale.

Another hobby I had was collecting cook books. This was an interesting hobby since I didn't do the cooking. I was very good at looking at recipes and picking out tasty-sounding things for my husband to make. Actually, I collected all kinds of books from classics to romance novels. Since I have always been an avid reader, the books just kept accumulating. Yes, I gave many away to other readers, but I had shelves and shelves filled with my books. When we downsized for the last time, friends that helped us move told me they never ever wanted me to buy any more books—or I could move them myself. Thankfully, the e-reader was invented and I was given one as a gift so I could quit buying hard or soft cover books. I do sneak one in now and then when something strikes my fancy. Turning the physical pages of a book is still my favorite reading method.

Fears

I was probably nine or ten years old when I became aware of the Cold War, and developed a strong fear of nuclear annihilation. There was a lot of talk about the Russians building H bombs that would blow us to smithereens and spew poisonous radioactive waste material into the atmosphere. Listening to news reports on our radio and hearing about movies depicting devastation and mutant creatures, put fear into my mind and the bottom of my stomach.

Air raid drills were held in school where you placed your head on your desk and placed your arms over your head. We had drills with "duck and cover" under desks, or we were herded into the basement, or were instructed on where the closest fallout shelter was located. Fallout shelters were areas designated all over the city as safe zones. Who knew if they were really safe, but the hysteria created by the media urged us to be alert to an atomic attack. When the sirens went off, one never knew if it was for real or just a test to feed the fear.

My husband's cousin built a bomb shelter in the basement of their house. We later purchased their house along with the Stejskal flower shop. The bomb shelter was constructed of cement blocks in a corner of the basement. A window to the area was removed and bricked in to provide a solid outside wall. Entrance to the shelter was through an L-shaped hall with a sharp turn, intended to block radiation into the main area, which was approximately 5 feet by 9 feet. Double bunk beds were built into one end. Shelving for food storage and containers for water, as well as waste, completed the shelter. No need ever occurred for its originally intended use, but it made a wonderful storm shelter, as well as a record storage vault.

Another building in the downtown area, occupied by a company I worked for, was also a designated shelter by the civil defense. Signs were displayed on buildings designated as fallout shelters for people to go to in the event of a nuclear attack. As an adult by then, I found it interesting that the building still had the drums for waste and water. This was in the 1970s. Since the drums were abandoned, we let employees take them for storage or burn barrels. These things always reminded me of my fears as a child.

Sample sign on buildings designated as safe shelters

Another big fear I had as a child was contracting the dreaded disease of polio. I don't remember how old I was when I became aware of our parents' concern for us in the summertime and their attempts to protect us. In our house, that meant no swimming in the creek. The public swimming pool was strictly off limits, as well as most public gathering places, since it was believed people contracted the disease from these areas.

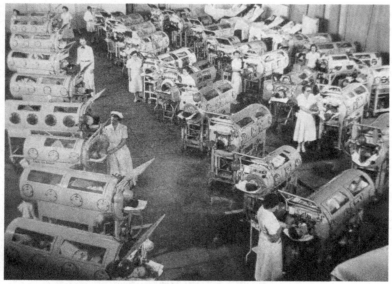

Pictures were broadcast of polio victims in iron lungs which was enough to strike fear in everybody, so the announcement of the first vaccine developed for widespread immunization was a welcome relief.

Even though the Cold War is technically over and polio has for the most part been eradicated in the United States, we continue to live under other types of fear. The latest one I heard about, which I will never have to fear, is "nomophobia," the fear of being without your cell phone.

HOLIDAYS

As children growing up, all holidays were important to us and were celebrated with family or friends in a traditional fashion. My husband could not understand how we always spent time with our family for all holidays. His family was not into sharing time with other family members, nor did they have many real traditions. I continued to carry on my family traditions, even adding some of our own. I hoped our children would carry them on, since many were a reflection of our Czech heritage, of which we are so proud.

Living on our acreage, as well as later owning our weekend house on the Mississippi River, provided the perfect venue for these holiday gatherings. Relatives and friends could be found at our house for most of these special occasions. Aunts and uncles, cousins and their families, would enjoy summer activities at the acreage.

Winter provided an opportunity for more formal dinners around the dining room table overlooking the tree-lined gullies. We often saw deer or wild turkeys roaming the area. No matter how busy we were in our small floral business, we always found a way to host these special get-togethers, which have provided many fond memories.

I have written my most memorable times for each of the major holidays as best as I can remember.

Easter

I bounced out of bed anxious to get dressed in my new Easter finery, and head to Babi and Deda's farm to celebrate this glorious holiday. The Easter bunny always stopped at the farm with lots of sweet treats, and hid colored eggs all over the fenced yard surrounding the house. All the cousins would be there, and I could hardly wait.

One year, Mom and Dad didn't want to disappoint me, but they told me to take a look outside—we weren't going anywhere. Overnight there had been an ice storm and everything was coated with sparkling ice, including the roads—not safe to travel. As I stood on the sofa looking out the living room window, I hoped for it to melt quickly, but that was not to be.

Beautiful to look at but not for traveling

My sister was still a baby so she didn't know the disappointment I was feeling. Mom tried to comfort me by saying we would have our own Easter Egg hunt at home with the eggs I had helped dye a few days before. It wasn't the same and not nearly as much fun, but I survived the day even though I never forgot the disappointment caused by Old Man Winter.

As I grew older I continued to look forward to this special holiday. I became involved in a church I attended with my best friend's family, and was baptized and confirmed as a member on Palm Sunday the year after I turned twelve. I loved all the significant ceremonies and bible stories, as well as the joyous music sung by the choir. Each year was better than the last.

After I had a family of my own, we continued the tradition of coloring and decorating eggs for the Easter Egg hunt.

Our son, Brent, helping his young cousin, Mallory, decorate the eggs

My husband's family joined in the festivities which included hanging salami in the tree for Deda, something special for Babi, and funny little gifts for the other adults. By this time we were living on an acreage so had plenty of area to cover. Depending on weather, the kids would fly kites and enjoy outdoor games. Eventually they became too grown up to be interested in dyeing and decorating real eggs, so the Easter Egg hunt became one of plastic eggs filled with money. This kept them interested instead of candy for several years.

Memorial Day

As a child Decoration Day, now known as Memorial Day, was a time to remember the men and women who died while serving in our country's armed forces. We also remembered family members and special friends who were no longer with us. This was done by placing flowers on their graves. We usually picked the flowers from our yard, hoping the peonies or lilacs would be in bloom. Our friend's dad across the road grew a field of gladiolus, which could also be cut if they were ready in time. The flowers were generally put into quart glass fruit jars or large food or coffee cans with the labels scrubbed off before taken to the cemetery. American flags were also placed by the Boy Scouts or veterans on the individual graves of the soldiers.

We would visit the Bohemian National Cemetery where most of our relatives were buried, going from grave to grave placing our remembrances. How beautiful the cemetery always looked with its newly mowed grass and neatly trimmed stones. I did not know that the man I would later marry was the son and grandson of two generations of caretakers of that cemetery. They took much pride in keeping it beautiful.

Text of "Neighbors" article from *The Gazette*:

Joe Stejskal figures he has about 6,500 people under him at work, and not one of them gives him any trouble.

Joe is caretaker of Czech National Cemetery. And he treats his 35 acres of sod and stone as if it were his own front yard. He keeps the grass as well-groomed as a golf course. And if Joe spots an overturned flower pot, it'll be upright before the day ends.

It's understandable that Joe takes such pride in the cemetery... It's been a part of his life since he was just a toddler. His father took care of the cemetery when Joe was growing up. "I remember going with my dad out in the country with a horse and wagon to get sod to cover the graves,"

Joe recalled. "I wouldn't get out of the wagon because I was afraid of cattle."

After reaching adulthood and working several years with his dad, Joe became chief caretaker in January 1952 when his dad retired.

Of course, Joe has a lot of memories from all his days with the cemetery—like the couple of occasions when he sold a plot, only to have the buyer commit suicide within a few days. He also recalled a time when he hired a fellow to dig up a grave and move a coffin, only to have the fellow quit in the middle of the project. "When the spade hit the top of the box, that guy scrambled out of that grave and said, 'I'm leaving.' He was through...just couldn't take it," Joe said.

A more recent memory of Joe's was the winter before last when the city received record amounts of snow. "That January was terrible...and I had 18 funerals that month," Joe said. "I was out here day and night checking the burners (used to thaw the ground in order to dig the grave). There was so much snow that even the tractors got stuck. And then we had a burial right where we'd been piling the snow. So we had to move the pile of snow.

"I really get a lot of credit from people (for keeping the cemetery in good shape). That really makes all the hard work worthwhile."

Joe, who lives at 2314 Southland St. SW, is naturally very familiar with the cemetery. In fact, he knows where almost all of its 6,500 inhabitants are buried. "One of the funeral directors tests me once in a while," he pointed out. "He'll name a person buried here and check to see if I can tell him where that grave is located."

At age 63, Joe naturally has to think about retirement, even though "I sure hate the thought of quitting. It's so darn nice out here...so peaceful, birds singing," he said. "I'd like to find a young fellow who would really take a lot of interest in the place and break him into the job. But, I can't

*find one. The benefits are better with a factory job. So most
young fellows go to work there."*
    [End of newspaper article].

There was a parade in the morning with several bands that
marched from downtown Cedar Rapids and up the C Street
hill to the cemetery. This was followed by a gathering of
people in the cemetery hollow. My family didn't stay for the
gathering. I have been told there was a stone wall which
acted as a stage for singers and dancers. Speeches were made
by veterans, politicians, religious leaders, and other local
dignitaries—mostly speaking in Czech. Other families
brought picnic baskets full of food for this all-day affair, and
they ate their dinner on the grounds. Water was provided by
an elevated waist-high metal trough hooked up to a water
faucet, not in plastic bottles, and canvas walls were built to
shelter bathroom facilities. Decoration Day was more like a
family reunion.

As I ponder Memorial Day, my thoughts gravitate to
our former flower shop business and the number of sales
made in both silk and fresh flowers. Many were made to the
same customers year after year, who continued to follow
their traditions of remembering. Since we were located so
close to the cemetery, now known as the Czech National
Cemetery, we provided many of the decorations, including
those required by the cemetery's "special care fund."

This meant getting up right after sunrise, loading the
van with flowers to be placed on the various family graves
before the service program began and people started their
visitation. This was a very stress filled time since we hoped
for good weather and also that these fresh flower bouquets
would meet the approval of the families.

I remember one particular Memorial Day getting a
call in the middle of the afternoon from a lady crying that
she didn't like the baby's breath (a filler-type flower) in her

81

bouquet and could we come and fix it. At that time we were living on the acreage but my husband drove back into town to fix her bouquet by removing the baby's breath and making her happy. Never did we add baby's breath to her flowers thereafter.

Decoration Day was later renamed Memorial Day and was changed from its traditional date of May 30th to the last Monday in May in order to create a three-day weekend. One has to wonder if this has taken away from the observance of Memorial Day and looked upon as the start of summer for camping, swimming pool openings, and related outdoor activities, as well as the running of the Indianapolis 500 on the Sunday preceding the holiday. I am still reminded of this special day of remembering, and make my trip to the cemetery visiting the graves of family members and refreshing memories of times gone by.

I recently read that in 2000 Congress passed the National Moment of Remembrance Act, asking people to stop for one minute at 3:00 PM and remember those that died in service to the United States. I wonder how many people really do this.

Fourth of July

Fourth of July, originally known as Independence Day, celebrates the adoption of the Declaration of Independence and the separation of the Thirteen Colonies from Great Britain. It is a national holiday celebrated on July 4th every year, one of the few holidays not always giving us a three-day weekend. It usually involves family reunions, concerts, barbecues, picnics, parades, baseball games, and fireworks.

Fireworks were a big part of the celebration for me. As a young child, I looked forward to an annual picnic that occurred at a different family home rotating amongst four of my mother's relatives. After returning home from this gathering, towards dusk, we would get together with the neighbors to shoot the big assortment of fireworks they always ordered from the back of comic books. We would drool over the different packages available and couldn't wait until my friend's dad placed the order and the postman would deliver them. There would be firecrackers, caps, snakes, sparklers, Roman candles, bottle rockets, fountains, mortar shells, lady fingers, and other loud explosives.

We were advised to be cautious of handling these fireworks, but as children we didn't always listen to the adults. One of the neighbor girls had a Roman candle explode backwards into her midriff causing a serious burn since she was holding it too close to her body. That didn't stop us from our fun which we continued until we had burned everything up and it was time to watch the big fireworks show that was held in the middle of the race track at Hawkeye Downs. We could see the fireworks from our front yard, except for the smaller ground displays.

Fireworks were illegal in Iowa but that didn't stop us from buying and shooting them off each year as part of our celebration on the Fourth. As we grew older, obtaining fireworks meant a trip to Missouri to purchase our stash. By this time, the boys we ran around with were into the really loud explosives known as silver salutes and M80s. They really packed a bang.

Early in our marriage, the Fourth of July meant camping with friends at Coralville Reservoir, and of course, fireworks. Even back in the early sixties, experimentation with blasting powder was something of interest to the guys. What a great time they had blowing up things with these more powerful firecrackers, until one exploded in the face of my husband. Thank goodness his eyeglasses prevented serious damage to his eyes, and he suffered only mild facial burns. Even though we were well aware of the dangers posed by firecrackers, we continued to obtain and discharge them year after year.

After we moved to the acreage, our annual picnic always included fireworks. The neighbor's dog was intrigued by the strings of small firecrackers and would try to pick them up to play with, so we had to watch her carefully. Our dogs were afraid of the noise and would usually be found hiding somewhere in the house. Even after we moved back into town and purchased our weekend home in Guttenberg, fireworks played a part in our celebration of the Fourth, although now they were being shot off from a dock over the Mississippi River.

Perhaps all those years of playing with fireworks have contributed to our current disinterest in the local displays. We are now content to hear them off in the distance without trying to fight the crowds of people gathered to watch the fiery displays over the Cedar River and surrounding towns.

Halloween

It was Halloween and all the neighborhood kids were excited about dressing up and trick or treating. Pumpkins were carved into scary jack-o'-lanterns with candles inserted. Scooping out the flesh was a yucky job, but was part of the tradition. A candle was inserted and lit for a flickering light. We were allowed to light our pumpkin several nights before Halloween so the candle had to be replaced almost daily. On Halloween it was left to burn completely down and more than once, pranksters would come by late in the night and smash our pumpkin.

The mothers were preparing for this special holiday by baking cookies, decorating cupcakes, making popcorn balls, and other sweet treats all wrapped in waxed paper and tied with black or orange curling ribbon. There was no concern for razor blades or pins and needles being inserted into treats for unsuspecting children. This was a different time. Purchased candy bars were a special treat given out only by the wealthiest neighbors. We knew which houses were the best houses to go to and which ones to avoid. In the days before Halloween, the major topic of conversation among the kids was, "What are you going as?"

Our costumes were all homemade, some more elaborate than others when the moms had the time or talent to sew. The only thing usually purchased was a mask. Selection of the mask set the tone for the entire costume, and it was with great excitement when we were able to go to Kosek's Dime Store on the "Avenue," (our main shopping area now known as Czech Village) to pick out the mask of our dreams. The masks were made of glazed paper, later plastic, with an elastic string attached to each side to slide over your head. There were holes in the mask for your eyes and openings made for your mouth. The masks were not very comfortable and usually were pulled up to the top of your head so you could see in the dark, and then pulled down when you reached your destination porch and knocked or rang the doorbell for the chanted "trick or treat."

We carried our paper bags from the grocery store which we had decorated with colorful ghost and goblin drawings, hoping to get them as full as possible. Halloween was a night for staying up late, and since we lived on the edge of town, almost like in the country, we quickly finished our neighborhood rounds. If we were lucky, one of our parents would load us up in their car and take us into a town neighborhood where the houses were closer together. It was usually a neighborhood where a friend or family member lived, but gave us a chance to get even more loot.

As we grew older, the treating was no longer part of the celebration, but the tricking became of more interest. In our neighborhood, indoor plumbing was just becoming available, so many homes still had "outhouses." It was a common practice to have them tipped over on Halloween. It was also a great prank to fill a paper bag with manure or dog poo, light it on fire on a person's porch, knock or ring the doorbell, run off to a safe spot, and watch them stomp it out getting the stuff all over their shoes. This was usually done to the stingiest people. We avoided real unruly behavior or pranks which would be especially destructive to anyone's property, but tried to think up things designed for fun and pranking beyond the expected pumpkin smashing.

My mother was a fun-loving person who enjoyed every holiday. One particular Halloween, after the ghosts and goblins were off the street, she dressed up as an old man in overalls, a bulky jacket, and a hat covering her hair down to her eyebrows. She removed her glasses and dentures (known as false teeth back then) and proceeded to hit the neighborhood. My sister and I tagged along since helping her see without her glasses was an important part of our job. Most people opening their door were very wary of this odd-looking man and quickly closed their doors. Our last neighbor to be visited was one of our best friends. My sister and I hid in the bushes while Mom climbed the steps of their porch. It was hard to keep from giggling as she pounded hard on the front door. The porch light came on as it had been turned off after the young trick or treaters were finished, and the door opened. Mom pushed her way into their house to their astonished and frightened looks, and said in her gruffest voice—"I want beer." The neighbors didn't know who she was or what to think, but it wasn't long before Mom couldn't keep from laughing and gave herself away. My sister and I climbed out of the bushes and went inside to join the party.

Mom pulled her teeth and glasses out of her pocket so she could properly celebrate. The adults drank beer; the kids had apple cider. Everyone had a good time laughing about the old man and his beer—a memory talked about to this day.

Sally and Ken enjoying Halloween

We continued our Halloween celebrations as adults usually at home parties with friends. Other times involved dressing my husband as a long-haired character knocking on doors of older friends or family, pushing his way into their homes, and scaring the dickens out of them, since he was not recognizable. We looked forward to Halloween. It was a fun holiday.

Thanksgiving

Something smelled really good as I woke on Thanksgiving morning. Mother was in the kitchen preparing a dish to take to Babi and Deda's farm for our family Thanksgiving get-together. All of their six children and their families congregated at the farm for every major holiday. The living room would be opened up to provide more room, and if the weather was cool, the oil burner stove would be lit to take the chill off. Babi would roast the turkey with stuffing inside, peel and mash the potatoes with freshly churned butter, make gravy, and bake pumpkin pies to be served with real whipped cream. The rest of the meal was brought by the family members, and included rolls made from scratch, sauerkraut from the fall canning, wild rice casserole, sweet potatoes, and other delicious treats.

One of my aunts always brought my favorite sweet treat, known as blarney stones, a white cake cut in bar-sized pieces, and rolled in a powdered sugar frosting and crushed salted peanuts. Of course, there were always kolaches with all different filings as well, including another favorite of mine, cottage cheese.

After Babi and Deda could no longer host the growing family, holiday gatherings were moved to the youngest daughter's farm. Her house wasn't large but it was newer and more modern, with a finished basement where a long table was set up to seat everybody. I mostly remember this aunt raised capons, which is what she roasted instead of turkey. A capon is a male chicken or rooster that has been castrated before reaching maturity. It was fed a special diet to improve the quality of meat and its size. It is not common to see capons in the grocery store much anymore, but they are heavy to the white meat and juicy and tender.

As the nieces and nephews or grandchildren grew up, married, and had families of their own, they developed their individual family holiday traditions. We had built a large home in the country to raise our family, and so it became the center for holiday celebrations for both my family and my husband's. We were not a large family but enjoyed our time together and the wonderful food served. Once parents were gone, children married and moved miles away, it became impractical to get everyone together. Some Thanksgivings were spent with just Ken's mom and the two of us, a somewhat lonely time of the year.

Christmas

Shhh, Santa is watching. It's getting close to Christmas and my sister and I are trying to be on our best behavior. Santa was known to peer in our windows after dark as Christmas was approaching. He would knock on a window, usually the kitchen window, and we would see his fur-trimmed hat and bearded face looking in at us and scaring us senseless.

We each had expressed our wants to the department store Santa. I so wanted that beautiful bride doll similar to the one I envied belonging to one of my friends. I didn't want to do anything that might be a deterrent from getting that special present. I tried to be especially good. We didn't get a lot of gifts from Santa, but he always tried to bring at least one thing of our heart's desire. He always filled our stockings with apples, candy, and nuts that needed a nutcracker to open. These were wonderful Christmas treats we always looked forward to. Sometimes a little storybook filled with Life Saver rolls of candy was tucked in our stockings. Our stockings were white cotton socks my dad wore. We wrote our names on them with a pen so Santa knew which one belonged to me and which one was Sandy's—just in case one of us got just a lump of coal.

The Christmas I wanted the bride doll remains a special memory, since my sister and I both had chicken pox.

Sally and Sandy

Dad brought in the usual evergreen tree he purchased from the warehouse where he worked. The challenge was to get it standing upright in the galvanized bucket filled with mud. We didn't have a fancy stand and dad wasn't an expert at building one like our German neighbor. Some trees were impossible to make stand properly, so they needed to be placed in a corner to lean against the wall for support. The lights were strung, a collection of ornaments were hung— many of which were handmade and stored from year to year. We strung popcorn garlands and made construction paper chains. Last of all, lots of silver tinsel was added to make the tree sparkle. We thought our tree was very beautiful. It

90

certainly was nothing like the magnificent decorations on trees today.

The gifts placed beneath the tree were mostly hand-made for family and friends. They were carefully wrapped in pretty paper and tied with crinkle ribbon bows. Our gifts were delivered by Santa on Christmas Eve. We were usually invited to one of our neighbor's or a friend's house for cookies, cheese and crackers, and some Christmas cheer. Lo and behold, when we returned home, Santa had been there and left our presents. We seemed to always just miss him. We would open our gifts on Christmas Eve, and Santa would return again during the night to fill our stockings, so we had something additional to look forward to when we woke up on Christmas morning.

Christmas Eve dinner traditionally consisted of an appetizer plate of crackers with head cheese, schulz, and pickled herring, followed by oyster stew. The first Christmas our Baba came to stay with us, she had never tasted oysters. I remember vividly her throwing them out of her bowl onto the table and calling out "zabi", meaning frog in Czech, and refusing to eat them. My mother was very upset with her since they were a delicacy to our family.

Because of the chicken pox that one particular year, we had to stay home. Mom had to run an errand and Dad stayed with us. There was a tap on the window and then a knock on our back door. My sister and I hung back, afraid to open it. Dad went to the door, and there stood Santa with a cloth bag of presents. I think it was actually a pillow case. Dad invited Santa in and he opened his bag and dug out presents for the whole family. We were so excited, we couldn't wait for our mom to get home so we could open our gifts. Shortly after Santa left, our mom returned and the celebration began.

Did I get my bride doll? Oh, yes I did. I loved her so much, straightening her veil and smoothing her dress. I made up stories about her marrying a handsome prince, until one day my sister decided to tear her head off. That was the end of the bride doll, which set me in tears. It was unable to be repaired and was discarded into the trash. My heart was broken and I really wanted to beat my sister up, but even though she was younger than I, she was more of a fighter. I was usually the one on the short end of the stick.

Santa came to our house every Christmas Eve until we were old enough to snoop, and found the Santa outfit and our presents hidden away in our mother's closet. Christmas just didn't have the magic it once had after that.

EDUCATION AND JOBS

Whenever I have talked to students or young people, I always encourage them to get as much education as they can regardless of the field they have chosen to work in. I never stopped learning and trying out new challenges, and scoffed at friends or people telling me, "I don't care if I never learn another new thing." What an awful way to think, since the world around us is full of new ideas and opportunities which makes life exciting for me.

Each of the jobs I held from the time of a young girl until retirement taught me something and contributed to my education. I think there is a story in each of those jobs which makes me the person I am today.

School and My Education

I turned five years old on September 20, 1946, and was ready to start school. It was an exciting place to go and I looked forward to walking back and forth each day with my friends. It was less than a mile, but in the winter it meant being bundled up in a snowsuit, boots, and a scratchy scarf tied around your face to keep the cold off. If you just wore blue jeans and got them wet from trudging through the snow banks in winter, you had to remove them once you got to school, hang them by the big old coal furnace to dry, and cover with a blanket until your clothes were dry enough to put back on. I was a shy little girl and would have been mortified if that happened to me, so I was very careful to stay out of the snow banks unless it was on the way home.

Our school had a vestibule with pegs to hang your coat or jacket and hat, and a shelf for your lunch pail, and where the water bucket and dipper sat. The water bucket was filled each day from a pump outside the school. The older students were given the task of filling the bucket with fresh water each morning.

Beyond this entrance hall was one large room. The teacher had her desk at the front of the room with a large blackboard behind her. White chalk was used to write on the blackboard and erasers were used to remove the writings. The erasers were cleaned by taking them outdoors and beating them against each other. Our desks were lined up in rows with one row for each grade—kindergarten through sixth grade. There were four students in my grade. Mrs. Dee was the teacher for all the grades and she instilled a love of reading and learning in each of her students.

Mrs. Dee with my friend Leslie from the neighborhood

A row of shelving ran across the back of the room which was filled with books appropriate for all grade levels. This was a magical place for me to visit when I had my lessons finished and I quickly became known as a bookworm.

We could check the books out to take home to read which I often did since books became an escape from reality for me. We had special activities and celebrations in school for all of the holidays. Mrs. Dee made sure school was a place of fun as well as learning. I remember a particular Halloween party where everybody dressed in costume and brought treats. My costume was homemade. I was supposed to be a cat. My mother dressed me in blue overalls, drew whiskers on my face, and pinned a rope tail on my butt. I was mortified and didn't want to go to school with this silly costume, but being poor, it was all I had. Most costumes were homemade, but it was the rope tail that bothered me the most. The treats were wonderful and included homemade cookies, cupcakes, popcorn balls, and candied apples, making the whole experience worthwhile. The games and the treats made me forget about that awful tail.

I attended the school known as Shaffer Heights through the fourth grade, when the powers to be, determined our little country school should be closed. The students were bused into town to the Taylor school from which I graduated after sixth grade. Mrs. Dee had done such a good job of teaching us, all her students were academically advanced over the "city kids," so school was easy for all of us.

An advantage of the new school was having an even bigger library, an art department, and a music department. Physical education in the old school was running up and down the hill behind the school to the outhouses at the top of the hill, or making up our own games in the grassy yard. Taylor school had a real playground with ball diamonds, basketball hoops, a jungle gym to climb on, and an ice rink in the winter to skate on or slide around, pushing people and falling down.

I loved art and drawing. For our sixth grade graduation ceremony, I was chosen to draw a picture I had created which was set to music. How proud and nervous I was on the big stage in my new $1 dress redrawing the picture for the audience while the music played. I mention the dollar dress because I had found it while shopping with my mom one day in Montgomery Ward's basement on a clearance table and thought it was the most beautiful dress. I begged my mom to buy it for me, which she did on the condition that it would have to meet the needs of being an Easter dress as well. It was orange taffeta and if you scraped it with your fingernail, it left a mark which was a permanent flaw in the material. This was the beginning of an interest in art which carried me all through school.

After grade-school graduation, we enrolled in Wilson High School which included students from seventh through twelfth grade. What fun it was to be involved in high school activities even though as seventh graders we had to sit on the floor of the auditorium during assemblies. There were organized sports, mostly for boys like track, baseball, football, basketball, and wresting, but being a spectator was just as much fun. Homecoming was a big deal with a huge pep rally and a bonfire out on the school yard. During the World Series, a television would be set up in the theatre so students could go in and watch during study halls if they had their work up to date. This was always an event to look forward to even if you weren't a fan of baseball.

As the student population grew, two new high schools were built—one for each side of the river. The two existing high schools on the west side of the city were turned into junior high schools and the tenth through twelfth graders were combined into the new high school named Thomas Jefferson High School. This occurred during the second semester of my junior year so we were the first full graduating class from the new high school in 1959.

I was involved in many activities in school from modeling to city government. I was editor of the class yearbook in my senior year and a writer for the school newspaper. I was an active participant in the art department headed up by Mr. Thompson. He was a big supporter of mine and selected my pieces of clay for submission to a committee at the University of Northern Iowa called Iowa State Teachers College back then. Apparently, my talent was sufficient for them to offer me a four year scholarship to the college. In 1959 this was quite an achievement for a poor "nerdy" girl from the country, but I was unable to take advantage of the opportunity due to family circumstances at home.

My father wanted me to be a nurse since he had such admiration for those taking care of him during his lengthy accident recovery, but that was not at all appealing to me. Instead, I enrolled in and graduated from the Cedar Rapids Business College which was akin to attending a community college today. The only difference being that it was a private school with its mission to provide an education in the requirements for business. Students were all ages and from all walks of life. Some were trying to prepare themselves for a whole new career. Then there were those like myself, fresh out of high school, trying to obtain skills necessary to obtain a job in the business world. I learned shorthand, typing, bookkeeping, and business-related subjects.

A couple of girls became friends of mine—one in particular I really developed a strong friendship with and even accompanied me on the train to visit my fiancé at Fort Leonard Wood, Missouri. In addition to the standard business classes, we practiced the Palmer method of writing, and operating a ten-key adding machine. Computers, copiers, and dictating machines were not in existence.

The business college was located on Second Avenue SW, not far from the bridge. There was a row of businesses along the river with bars and restaurants as a place to go during our breaks from classes. Some of my friends and I would often go to one particular restaurant during our break, which is where I learned to drink coffee and smoke cigarettes. I would have only been nineteen at the time, but coffee and cigarettes were such an "in thing" to do and how adult we thought we were.

Over the years I took several classes at Kirkwood Community College as well as the University of Iowa. In spite of my success in the business community, my biggest regret was not going on to college and getting an academic degree in business.

Sally on the left next to Mr. Hunt

My Musical Education

I turned eleven years old, and like other students at a certain age, it was time to learn to play a musical instrument. The instrument of choice for Czech families was usually the accordion. I began taking piano accordion lessons at Kinney Studios in downtown Cedar Rapids. The studio specialized in guitar and accordion lessons and was located in a space on second floor of an old building. I can't say I really enjoyed my lessons, but I practiced faithfully and climbed the wooden stairs dragging my accordion in its case up to the second-floor studio each week for my lesson.

I have never been musically inclined. I could not hold a beat, had two left feet, and carrying a tune was way beyond me, but I gave the accordion my best effort until my first recital. I practiced the selected music over and over until I knew it by heart and could play it without mistakes. The recital was held at the Paramount Theatre, so I packed up my accordion, wore my best outfit, and was taken to the theatre by my parents. I did not pack my sheet music in my accordion case since I was confident I knew it from start to finish.

As I waited back stage for my turn to go on, I suddenly realized I could not remember a single note of how to perform the piece I was selected to play. I could not refresh my memory no matter how hard I tried—it was a total blank. I had no sheet music to help me remember. I entered the stage at my turn and tried to force it, pressing the buttons, playing piano keys, and expanding the bellows in and out, but as you can imagine, it was awful, and I was totally humiliated. I don't remember ever having another recital, so I must have given up playing the accordion except for an occasional beer barrel polka for my parents and their friends. My disastrous stage performance taught me a life lesson about being overconfident

Sally with her accordion.

In junior high school you were required to have at least one semester of music. Since I didn't play an instrument appropriate for band or orchestra, that left the only other choice: choir. As a singer, I couldn't—and still can't—hold a tune on a platter. I entered the class full of trepidation, but knew I had to get through it the same way I attacked other projects—find a way to do the best I could.

Singing as a group in chorus was a great way to hide my anxiety, but then came time for the final test for our grade. Each student had to sing solo for the teacher, while standing in front of the entire class. With my voice quivering and my knees shaking, I got through the song with all eyes upon me and without their ears covered up. I prayed I would get a decent grade when report cards were finally distributed for the semester. I cautiously peered inside and my heart fell to my feet when a big letter "C" jumped out at me for music. This was amongst all the A's which were the norm for me. I had never received a "C" in my entire school life, so was glad that semester was over and never needed to be repeated. I was done with music!

The next chapter in my musical training related to dancing. Even as a child I don't remember a lot of music and dancing in our house. I do remember going to the ZCBJ and CSPS Czech social halls with my parents. Occasionally I played with other kids along the side lines or upstairs at ZCBJ, peering over the railing overlooking the main floor where a band played and our parents danced. I remember they danced to a lot of polkas, waltzes, and the two step.

In junior high we were being taught how to square dance. Most kids, especially the boys, hated it, but I thought it was fun. Even with two left feet I could follow the calls and enjoyed doing the do-si-do.

This was about the time friends would gather together at different houses on weekends for parties. Basements were decorated with crepe paper streamers, a record player was set up with the latest songs playing. Kids would often bring some of their own records so there was always a good choice of music to dance to. This was another area of expertise I was lacking in. I preferred to sit on one of the folding chairs positioned along the side of the dance area, probably closest to the food. Parents hosting the party always supplied a great selection of things to eat. One of our best parties was at the home of a friend, Fred Russo, whose dad started the restaurant known as Leonardo's and introduced us to pizza. This was the first time most of us had ever tasted this interesting pie. That party will always be remembered as a milestone in our culinary taste which is still enjoyed today.

Since dancing was difficult for me, I begged my Mother for dancing lessons which I believed would solve the problem of two left feet. The only lessons available were from the Arthur Murray studio, so I was enrolled. As I climbed the wooden stairs to the second floor above the Paramount Theater, I fervently hoped these lessons would help me turn into a dancer instead of a tin soldier with stiff joints and a pounding heart. Oh, they tried to teach me the tango, the waltz, the mambo, and other ballroom dances, but that was not what my friends were doing. Rushing home after school, everybody was watching the TV show, "American Bandstand." In our poodle skirts and saddle shoes, we bought the latest rock and roll records and copied the dance fads like the twist, the jitterbug, and the stroll, plus variations of more classic dances. I watched all the moves, but I was just not meant to be a dancer. I continue to sit on the sidelines to this day.

"Carousel" was the theme of the Wilson high school sophomore class dance Friday evening in the school gymnasium. Pictured above, from left, are Charles Hackman, 2033 Burlington street SW, class president; Stella McArthur, 1807 N street SW, program chairman; Sally Auerbrenner, 3529 Southland street SW, class secretary-treasurer, and Ken Stejskal, 2230 C street SW.

104

Learning to Drive

I was sixteen years old, and like any other teenager of that age, I was excited about getting my driver's license. Even though I could not afford a car of my own, being able to drive the family car would allow me to not always be dependent on other people for rides. It would give me a certain amount of freedom, even though our family car was old. In spite of its age, my father always took good care of his vehicles and it was a standing joke that he was going to wash, wax, and polish the finish off.

In order to get my driver's license, I was required to take driver's education in school. It was offered as a special elective to all students who met the age requirement. Besides the written handbook of rules for the road, we practiced driving in a realistic car-driving simulator. I thought this was great fun similar to playing a video game today. Once you were proficient using the simulator, we were taken out to drive with an instructor in a brand new Edsel with an automatic transmission. We felt very fortunate to have a new car to practice driving in, not realizing or caring that this car would become one of the worst cars of all time, and one of Ford Motor Company's largest failures.

By this time, I had a learner's permit, and after passing all the driver tests in school, I was ready to apply for my license with the Iowa Department of Motor Vehicles. This meant driving with one of the state examiners. I was nervous about failing the test. For some reason, when I showed up to take my final driver test, they accepted my paperwork from school, took my picture, and issued my driver's license. All that worrying was for naught. I have never had to take a driver test since, although after that certain age which I am fast approaching or perhaps even approached, I may be selected to take one. At my latest renewal after my 74th birthday, I tried to look perky and not limp when I entered the DOT offices. So far I have even been able to pass the vision test without my glasses, so I am proud of not being restricted, since I often remove them for driving after dark. I have, on more than one occasion, let my license expire and was required to take the written test, but this was entirely my fault for not paying attention to the expiration date.

I was so proud to have my driver's license, I begged to drive our car whenever I could. I remember one incident in particular related to my inexperience as a driver. It was winter and I had taken my dad to work, since I needed the car that day. It was time to pick him up. I was running late, so was driving too fast for the icy road conditions. As I started down the lengthy Bowling Street hill, the car lost traction and began sliding to the left and then back to the right, hitting the curb and back left again. I over-corrected, just barely missing a car coming up the hill. Reaching the bottom of the hill and finally getting the car under control, I took a deep breath, and needed to change my underwear. I thanked God for allowing me to escape what could have been a serious accident. That experience remains in my memory to this day when driving conditions are treacherous.

After getting a driver's license, everyone's next dream is to have their very own car. It took me until 1960 to get mine. My grandparents on the farm were auctioning their possessions after selling the beloved family farm and moving to town. I decided to bid on their car, a 1946 Ford which I won the bid on for $150 and became the proud owner of my first car. I had to have my boyfriend drive it home for me since it was a manual shift and I hadn't learned how to drive a "stick." After many jerks and starts and stops, I finally got the hang of it. Proudly I drove my very own car to my job in downtown Cedar Rapids.

I was married in 1961 and when moving to California, sold my old car to a hunter to use in driving into backwoods areas. It was sad to say good-by to that old car, but my new husband had a brand new vehicle to enjoy instead.

Early Jobs

I was nine years old and eager to earn some money of my very own. One of my neighborhood friends knew of a truck farmer that hired kids to help harvest their produce. It was strawberry picking season and I quickly signed up, excited to have a real job. We had to walk a little over a mile to the pickup station at the closest high school, where a big truck with high wooden sideboards would come by at 7:00 am to load all the workers and take us to the farm.

Once there, we were given carriers holding six quart boxes to hold the strawberries. We crawled along our assigned rows picking the strawberries. You could eat as many as you wanted, but then your boxes would not fill up as fast. I loved strawberries, so I ate a lot of them. When the carrier was filled, you would take it to the collection station and would be given a ticket for each quart filled, and a new set of empty boxes. At the end of the week, you turned your tickets in for your pay at the rate of five cents per quart.

It was hot crawling on your knees all day in the burning sun, but eating lunch packed in a black metal lunch pail was a pleasant break in the day. A pretty little creek ran through the farm and we would remove our shoes and socks, sit on the bank, and dangle our feet in the water to cool off while eating our lunch. Back to the fields to continue picking until the final call at 5:00 pm to turn in our picks and get our pay tickets. We would then climb back into the truck for the ride back to the school and the long walk home after a full day in the fields.

I remember thinking this was a hard way to make a living—low pay for awfully hard work, and besides, I firmly believed the farm owner didn't like me. I must not have been a fast-enough producer, often sidetracked by baby bunnies in my picking row, or other critters and insects I seemed to find. I even took one of those baby bunnies home in my lunch pail, thinking I could feed it from an eyedropper and raise it to be a pet. My dad warned me it would not work, and he was right. Little did I know that bunny needed his cozy nest and the warmth of his mother to survive.

In any event, why did I think the farmer's wife didn't like me? I was always given the rows previously picked and had the smallest berries, so it took much longer to fill my boxes while the picker "pets" were assigned the newer planted rows with the big plump juicy berries.

As I contemplated this situation over the weekend break and counted my meager pay for the week, I had a great idea on how to increase my production. I could hardly wait to begin my job the following Monday. As usual, I was assigned the oldest and least productive picking row, but I had a plan—fill the bottom of the boxes with straw from between the rows and pick enough strawberries to cover the straw and round off the top of the quart boxes. I quickly filled my boxes and turned my carrier in for my share of pay tickets. I was pleased with myself since I had my most productive day.

At the end of the day before climbing into the truck, the farmer's wife called me over to the collection station, asked for my tickets, paid me and said, "Don't come back." I was fired from my first real job, but I learned a valuable lesson about doing a job properly.

108

Failing as a strawberry picker, I still needed to find a means of making some spending money, so babysitting neighborhood kids became a way. Like my friends, I was reaching the age of wanting to buy things when we went shopping downtown to McClellans Dime Store, Kresge's, or Woolworths. I mostly babysat on weekends when parents wanted to go out. The summer following my eleventh birthday, my mother took me to interview with a family on the southeast side of Cedar Rapids. Mrs. Bell liked me and agreed to hire me for the summer, taking care of her three kids and helping around the house. Little did I know what helping around the house meant.

Dana was seven or eight, Jimmy was five, and little Johnny was only a year and a half old—still in diapers. I went to work on Monday morning, walking to the nearest bus stop at Wilson School, and taking the bus to 1st Avenue and 29th Street SE. I then walked to the Bell's house on Country Club Drive across from the Cedar Rapids Country Club golf course. I stayed with the Bells all week going home on Friday, unless they needed me on the weekend, which was a little extra pay. I was paid $15 a week.

Mr. Bell, John—everyone called him Jack—traveled a lot for the family company, Bell Construction Equipment. Mrs. Bell, known as Skippy, played a lot of golf, spent a lot of time at the Cedar Rapids Country Club swimming pool, and was involved in many other social activities.

I was responsible for getting the children up and dressed, preparing their breakfasts, and entertaining them for the day. For a long time, I could not imagine eating pancakes, waffles, or French toast because those were their breakfasts of choice.

Dana would go off to play with the little Hoyt girl next door, Jimmy had a friend at Skogman's just a couple of houses away, so it was usually just Johnny and me. I mention these family names because they are still a significant part of the Cedar Rapids business community. After feeding the kids lunch, loading the dishwasher—an amazing appliance to me—little Johnny napped. I usually had a basket of Jack's white shirts to iron. If it was really, really hot, Mrs. Bell would let me iron in their very large bedroom on the second floor, because it had a window air conditioner. What a welcome relief it was from doing the ironing in the hot downstairs dining room. Those white shirts were cotton and had to be sprinkled with water to make them damp so the iron would get the wrinkles out. To sprinkle them, I used a pop bottle with a stopper filled with holes on the top.

Dana was a sweet little girl and I slept in her bedroom when I stayed there. Her bedroom was very large compared to mine at home. I shared my bedroom at home with my sister. It was so small, I had to climb over one army bunk to get to the other. Dana's room was beautifully decorated with window seats overlooking the neighborhood and golf course. It was a great place to sit and read. The twin beds were made up with lovely linens and matching turquoise bedspreads that were monogrammed with a big fluffy D against a denim-type fabric. Once the boys were settled for the night, Dana and I would read, play games, and my favorite girlie thing—paint finger and toenails.

A couple of incidents remain fixed in my memory—both having to do with fingernail polish. This was a luxury we didn't indulge in at my house, so I felt like being in the lap of luxury when Dana and I would paint our nails. I was sitting on my bed and she accidentally brushed a wet fingernail against the beautiful bedspread. I knew we would be in big trouble, so when I made the beds the next morning, I switched the bedspreads so the one with the polish smear would be against the wall. This went undiscovered until Mrs. Bell came in one day to change the linens and noticed the stain. Dana was blamed for it, but I had to fess up to it being my fault and switching the bedspreads accidentally, I said.

110

We both got lectured, but Mrs. Bell got over her anger and life went on.

The second incident occurred when Mrs. Bell decided to reward me and the children by taking us to the Cedar Rapids Country Club for dinner one night. Can you imagine how exciting that sounded to this poor girl from the southwest side of town by the railroad tracks. I polished my well-worn sandals, picked out my best summer outfit that I had with me, and decided to polish my toe nails, only this time in the upstairs bathroom. In my haste to get them done and my nervousness about the upcoming dinner—oops, I dropped the bottle of nail polish which spilled all over the bathroom rug. How was I ever going to explain that to Mrs. Bell. I tried using nail polish remover, but the stain was too large and the remover just made it spread out more. I tried washing the rug, but that didn't work either. There was nothing else to do but confess to Mrs. Bell when she got home. With tears running down my face, I explained what happened, apologized, and was sure she would cancel our special dinner. Instead, she hugged me and said it was okay, she needed to replace the rug anyway. What a lady!

I have to say, that dinner was something to remember. We were seated in the dining room of the Country Club amongst Cedar Rapids elite members. There were linen-covered tables with cloth napkins, fresh flower centerpieces, and soft lighting. I felt like I was in heaven, even with my worn-out sandals and shabby clothes. The dinner was magnificent. Mrs. Bell ordered King Crab for herself and me, which I had never seen before, let alone eaten. It was wonderful and continues to be one of my favorite meals to this day.

The Bells were very kind to me, and often provided special experiences which were beyond my expectations. Mr. Bell had his own small airplane which he used for business pursuits, as well as his personal love of flying. One weekend he took me to Hunter Field, a small airfield at the south edge of Cedar Rapids, and took me up in his airplane. What an exciting experience that was overlooking the city and rising above the clouds.

I worked for the Bells every summer until I was sixteen and was hired by the Cedar Rapids Department of Recreation. Once I was hired by the city, I spent time after school and on Saturdays at the Riverside Recreation Center located in Riverside Park. This was an old fire station turned into a neighborhood rec center where the kids could come to play table tennis, shoot pool, do crafts, and other organized activities. I helped the full-time director making sure the kids checked in and out, as well as helping with any activities he needed a hand with.

One of the special kids I got to know and love came every day. His name was Henry, but we called him "Hank." Hank was what was known back then as retarded. He was actually over 40 years old, but played with all the other kids that came to the center. Hank was special and got along with everyone. He held a special place in my heart, and he was very upset when the center closed after a couple of years.

After the center closed, the city transferred me to the Ellis Park swimming pool. I started in the basket room and then worked into being the cashier. This was a great summer job and I was paid $1 an hour—great pay for a teenager back then. Another perk was the after-closing parties in the pool. We could swim and play as long as one of the life guards wanted to stay on duty.

While going to business college I worked part-time at Killian's, a downtown department store. My first assignment was making bow after bow in their dingy storeroom during the Christmas season for the gift-wrap department.

At Easter I was assigned to their annex building in the toy department sitting on a throne as the Easter bunny. The costume was beautiful and brand new. Getting in and out of the outfit was time consuming. I could remove my

112

head and gloves in order to eat my lunch in a private little alcove of the store overlooking the street. Having lunch provided was a real bonus to the job, and I looked forward to seeing what the kitchen was sending up to me. The kitchen at Killians provided wonderful food, and many shoppers as well as downtown business people came there to eat.

While on duty, I sat on a raised platform beautifully decorated in vibrant colors, and talked to the children as they came up to see me. I had a basket of treats to hand out, and when there were no children present, the most fun was sitting perfectly still while an adult was browsing the store, and then waving at them when they least expected me to be alive and scaring them out of their wits. The above picture includes a little girl with the bonnet, who would years later become my sister-in-law. There were fifteen years difference between my husband and his little sister.

I later upgraded my job to running the passenger elevator with its metal cage and manual up and down handle. My elevator goal was to operate it without jerks, and to stop level with each floor. I really enjoyed all these jobs at Killians. During breaks, I could roam the store daydreaming about all the wonderful products from clothing, furniture, cosmetics, toys, sporting goods, and stationery. There was even a candy counter and a full restaurant. Downtown department stores were magical buildings in which to shop. It was very sad to see them close and be replaced by the trend towards mall shopping.

BECOMING AN ADULT

I remember when I couldn't wait to be an adult. That meant living away from home, making my own decisions, and being totally independent. Once that day came, I had to ask myself if that was what I really wanted. As usual, I pushed forward gathering new experiences and meeting life head on.

Friends

One of my best friends in high school was Carol Ann. For some reason which I have forgotten, we always called her by her first and middle name. Carol Ann had an older sister in college who we didn't see often, a brother three or four years older than we were, and a younger brother. Her older brother was named Ken, but everybody called him Shorty. His passion was motorcycles. Shorty was a scramble track racer and every weekend we would jump into Carol Ann's parent's car and head to wherever he was racing. We became friends with many of the other racers and their families, especially those with sisters our age. After the races, we would usually spend the night at Carol Ann's home, since it was in town and a gathering place for many of Shorty's friends. If we were lucky, they would take us cruising on the backs of their motorcycles.

Scramble races were held all over the country, but Shorty and his buddies mostly raced in the Midwest. Scramble tracks were usually built in a remote area of a community. They included marked laps through wooded areas, hills, creek beds, gullies, mud, rocks, ruts, and other rugged terrain. The riders were tested on their skill and endurance, as well as their ability to maintain the highest speed throughout the race, which consisted of a certain number of laps. The competitors typically rode English bikes, Triumphs being the most popular, followed by BSAs and Nortons. Harley Davidsons had not come into their popularity at this time and were considered to be "hogs" because of their bulk and weight. As spectators we lined the race track standing far enough back to not get hit or run over by a wayward bike.

Carol Ann and I had our own cheering section for our favorite riders. Besides Shorty, there was a Bob, two Bills, and a Denny. Denny preferred flat track racing which ultimately led to his death. All of these racers were amateurs, and competed for trophies in their different classes according to experience and the size of their motorcycle engines. When this group of guys were not racing on the scramble tracks, they took up hill climbing, another form of motorcycle competition on a steep hill trying to reach the top in the shortest amount of time. Hill climbs are still held in the same area near Anamosa, Iowa.

Our love of motorcycle racing and the group of friends that went with it, evolved into some pairing off with the particular racers. Each of the guys had racing bikes as well as street bikes. How fun it was to be riding behind one of them down the highway at speeds in excess of ninety miles per hour—your hair blowing in the wind, sandals or tennis shoes on your feet, and no protective gear. It makes me shudder thinking about it now. It's a wonder not one of us was killed or in an accident that would maim us for life.

Carol Ann learned to ride one of her brother's smaller motorcycles. One spring day while we were seniors in high school, the weather was just too nice to stay in school. We gathered our books and left the school to go to her house and take the "bike" for a ride. How smart we thought we were cruising the loop downtown, Carol Ann driving, and me riding on the back. Stopping at a red light on First Avenue East, waiting for the signal to change. The light changed to green. Carol Ann accidentally popped the clutch, we did a wheelie, and down we went. How embarrassing it was, since a police car was in line right behind us. Of course he pulled over to check if we were hurt, checked her license, and helped us right the bike so we could proceed on our way. This incident totally deflated our enthusiasm for our ride.

We returned back to the house and had to explain to Shorty about the dings on his motorcycle. Of course we were severely admonished about taking his bike without permission. That was the last of the rides I remember with Carol Ann driving.

We remained friends throughout high school. I was her maid of honor at her wedding. After my wedding, we continued our friendship as couples until they moved west. Our life styles changed, sadly caused us to drift apart, leaving only the memories.

There were many adult friends over the years, two of them are now gone, but remain in my memory. One was from the Island in Guttenberg. Sheri raised four children—two boys and two girls, and lost another son at birth. She had many challenges in her life, many disappointments and heartaches. She managed to stay balanced, immersed in her faith, and avoided complaining. She always remained positive and never had a bad word to say about anyone, regardless of their feelings for her. They sometimes raised their heads in jealousy or some other issue. I deeply admired her spirit and missed her terribly after she lost her battle with cancer.

My other special adult friend, Carol, was a horse of another color—brassy, outspoken, and known as "the bitch." We had been friends since early in our marriages. As couples we did a lot together until her husband had an unexpected heart attack while on vacation. He died after a few months of lingering in a bed-ridden capacity. Carol worked for me in the flower shop office two days a week. We were able to keep our friendship intact, sharing our innermost thoughts, fears, and lots of humor. She also succumbed to a surprise heart attack and is greatly missed. Below is her family.

Back row: Kevin, Scott   Front row: Marcy, Carol, Bob

First Time Bridesmaid

It was May, 1961, and my best friend through most of my school years was getting married. I was going to be her bridesmaid. My fiancée had just returned from basic training in the Army and would be the best man. We had been inseparable as couples all through high school and for several years after.

120

I had never been a bridesmaid before. We shopped for our dresses. The choice for the bridesmaids was a light blue satin dress with a V-neck down the back, short sleeves, and a large tulle bow with long tails attached at the tip of the V and overlaying the A-line skirt. I thought it was a beautiful dress and couldn't wait to wear it for the wedding with the high heel shoes of satin material dyed to match the dress color. I don't remember what we carried for flowers, but it was a beautiful sunny day in May, just perfect for a wedding.

I so was excited to be part of this event to be held in the church we both had attended from childhood. In fact, it was her parents who introduced me to Salem Evangelical United Brethren Church. My parents did not participate in any type of organized religion. I became involved in the church, going to Sunday school, studying the Bible, belonging to the youth group, eventually becoming baptized, taking communion, and becoming a member of the church. I really loved Reverend Deaver and his family, and even after he was transferred to another church outside of town, he returned to perform my own wedding.

On the day of my friend's wedding, we waited outside the church for the time to begin the procession. In my state of nervousness, I decided I needed to use the bathroom one last time. Down to the restroom in the church basement I went, did my duty, flushed, stood up and realized the tails of the tulle bow had been in the toilet and were dripping all over my shoes. Wringing out the tails, I hurried up the stairs, went outdoors fanning them in the breeze trying to get them to dry. Time was rushing by so we hurried over to the pastor's house next door to the church where his wife set up her ironing board and pressed the tails dry, with me still wearing the dress. The shoes were another matter, but I don't think anyone noticed the spots on them. The wedding proceeded on time, and we often laughed about the incident during anniversary celebrations.

Marriage and Army Life

While I was beginning a career in the banking business, Kenneth Joseph Stejskal, the young man I had dated all through high school was trying to figure out what he should do with his life, so he joined the army and headed to Fort Leonard Wood, Missouri for basic training. Several of our friends were getting married. We were planning a wedding after he completed his first six months of active duty as a medic at Fort Sam Houston in Texas. This was a specialized program followed by a six-year commitment in the army reserve which included monthly weekend meetings and two weeks of summer camp each year.

Morning exercises and second floor of barracks lived in

Home at Christmas for a short leave—at my house

With his little sister Kathy

Having camped in all types of weather with buddies, a winter bivouac was not expected to be a challenge. As soldier Ken prepared his tent to keep warm by piling snow all around, his drill sergeant would not let that be. He came around and kicked all the snow away from his tent to make the camping more uncomfortable.

Fort Sam Houston, Texas
Basic Training Graduation in Dress Uniform

125

On September 9, 1961, the hottest day of that year, I was married in the church without air conditioning. I had attended this church since I was a young child. The reception was held in Sokol Hall, too small for all the family and friends who were crowded in. It was the only venue available

on that date, and no air conditioning there either. The groom's family provided the food which was in abundance, and the beverages flowed to keep the attendees satisfied.

After sweating it out, we were finally able to leave the festivities for our honeymoon. We drove away in a beautiful new burgundy Chevrolet with burgundy fabric seats and interior. My husband was perspiring heavily, not only from the heat, but probably a case of nerves as well. The back of his white shirt turned burgundy. We laughed a lot as we happily headed for the beautiful Rocky Mountains, enjoying everything nature had to offer. We also visited an old high school friend stationed with the Air Force in Colorado Springs.

Upon our return home to a little three-room house we rented from my husband's parents, a letter was delivered from the Department of the Army ordering my husband to report for active duty in just a few days to Fort Ord in Monterey, California. Many reservists, especially those in specialized units, were being called to active duty as a result of the Berlin Wall crisis and a major flare up in the Cold War.

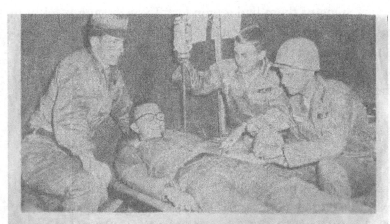

ON ACTIVE DUTY—Two Cedar Rapids men, members of the 301st field hospital unit now on active duty at Fort Ord, Calif., recently participated in an army training test. PFC Kenneth Stejskal, on stretcher, receives aid from PFC Jerry Maples (without hat) while PFC Darwin Bemer (left) of Milwaukee, and Wayne Johnson of Minneapolis look on. The 301st, commanded by Lt. Col. Elwood Buchman of Iowa City, has been on active duty six months.

Fox hole training on the firing range

Off he went to play war games while I stayed in our little house continuing to work at the bank. After graduation from business college I had been ready for a full-time job. I applied and was hired as a teller in the installment loan department of what was then known as Merchants National Bank. The department was small with only four loan officers and a half-dozen tellers and support personnel. I quickly became friends with the staff, including the loan officers.

One of them had a wonderful voice, sang weekly in his church choir, and agreed to sing at my wedding. Unfortunately, the day before our wedding he came down with a severe case of laryngitis, so the singing never occurred, but the wedding went on as planned.

I had some amazing experiences working in this department, including the firing of our head teller for embezzlement. She claimed to have only borrowed the money from her drawer overnight to pay for having her car fixed, but unfortunately for her, the bank auditors showed up that day to examine our accounts and discovered the shortage. We were all shocked and sorry for her. What a lesson learned by all.

Members of Lambda chapter of Beta Sigma Phi modeled at the fashion show for the "working woman" presented Wednesday night at Armstrong's. Mrs. Kenneth Stejskal, 52 Twentieth ave. SW, left, wears a tangerine brushed wool dress with a sash tie and a matching hat of fake fur. Mrs. Helen Jacobson of Shellsburg models a 3-piece costume of worsted and orlon. The gray skirt and sweater are topped by a yellow and gray plaid collarless jacket.

Once I entered the business world, working full time, I was invited to join the Lambda chapter of Beta Sigma Phi. This is a non-academic sorority, primarily acting as a social and cultural organization, incorporating service as part of its activities. I knew some of the women in the local chapter and admired them from my high school days. These were respected people in their various occupations, and great mentors for me. The success of these women intimidated me, but

129

also greatly inspired me to reach out and crawl out of my box.

I loved my job and was sorry to leave when my husband came home for Christmas leave and insisted I accompany him back to California. I missed my job and the Beta Sigma Phi meetings and programs when we moved to California. [When later we returned to Cedar Rapids, I did not renew my membership in the Lambda chapter, but am thankful for the part the ladies played in my career development.]

Many of the army wives were joining their husbands, so we packed as many belongings as would fit into our car and headed west, driving almost nonstop to reach his army base on time. We drove what was known as the southern route. The northern route was much shorter, but too risky weather-wise in the winter.

It seemed like the drive would never end since we only stopped for a short nap along the road or to get a bite of something to eat. I remember a particular stop for pizza in Oklahoma. Pizza was a fairly new type of food to us, having been introduced to it by a friend from high school whose dad owned one of the original pizza parlors in Cedar Rapids. We eagerly ordered a pizza with everything on it—big mistake. We did not know what everything meant, and it included anchovies, which neither of us had ever tasted before, and which neither of us wanted to taste again. Yuck—we ended up throwing it in a garbage can along the way, and proceeded on our way still hungry.

We finally arrived at our destination. After checking in at the army post, we had to quickly find a place to live on a private's salary of $62 per month. This would equate to $495 per month in 2015, so still not a lot of money. We didn't have much time to look so we found an apartment in a very old two-story house located in the town of Salinas. Salinas was a nice little town located in the valley and the heart of lettuce farming. The apartment was furnished, but

130

everything was dirty, old, and well used. We slept in our sleeping bags, not wanting to make up the bed holding a musty-smelling and stained mattress. The weather was particularly cold that year, so we huddled in our sleeping bags on a dingy couch, in a dark and even dingier living room watching the portable television we brought with us from home. Our budget was extremely limited so much of our entertainment consisted of watching TV, driving the seventeen-mile drive along the coast, or walking around the town of Carmel ogling the merchandise in the intriguing shops. One exception I recall was a particular gourmet food shop having chocolate-covered crickets and other insects for sale. This little Midwestern girl could not believe people actually ate bugs, chocolate-covered or not.

Our landlady lived next door and sat in her front window all day long watching whatever was going on in the neighborhood. I think she was handicapped because she never moved from her chair and we were a little afraid of her. Cooking in the apartment proved to be quite interesting. First of all, neither of us had much experience with cooking, and second, the oven in the old stove did not work. Trying to bake a pizza turned out to be a real challenge. Although microwaves were in existence, this was prior to their acceptance as a real cooking aid. Our cooking methods involved deep frying or cooking in an electric skillet, both wedding presents we brought with us.

Pepsi Cola was our drink of choice and the empty bottles accumulated in the kitchen, until one day we discovered an army of ants coming up the back staircase, which descended from the kitchen area to an alley behind the house. Having no knowledge of how to deal with ants, we remembered an old vacuum cleaner in the downstairs vestibule, brought it up and quickly sucked up all the ants. We were relieved to have solved that problem until the next day when we discovered all the ants were back. It finally dawned

131

on us that we needed to get rid of all the empty pop bottles. That, which along with little capfuls of poison scattered about, took care of the pesky ant problem.

As I mentioned, the house was very old and the weather was very cold when we arrived in what was supposed to be sunny California. The apartment was heated by gas wall heaters which did not produce much heat, but did take the chill off. We were watching the Bob Hope golf tournament one Sunday afternoon and noticed they began to talk about snow on the Pebble Beach Golf Course. Sure enough, we looked out our front window to see snow covering the sidewalks, cars sliding around, and children, without hats or mittens, trying to make snowmen. They were so excited playing in the snow while we were thinking they were crazy. We thought we had left that all behind in Iowa.

We both began to wake up with very bad headaches and couldn't figure out why. During one night, I woke up coughing and having trouble breathing. I flung open the bathroom window gasping for air and realized we were being gassed by a leaky heater. We did get the landlady to repair the heater but decided we got a lucky break to be alive. It was time for me to find a job so we could move. I was getting restless while my husband went to work. I had no place to go during the day, so I started my job search.

Most employers were reluctant to hire military people since they knew we were mostly temporary. For some reason, the Bank of America liked my references. They offered me a full-time job in their trust department. Our quest for new housing began in earnest. We often dreamt of living in an apartment complex which was relatively new at the edge of town. It was built in a Spanish style, and we were sure it would be out of our price range, but we decided to check their sign that advertised an apartment for rent anyway. The owners were a delightful Italian mother and son. When they came to meet us and saw where we were living,

I think they took pity on us and agreed to rent us a one-bedroom apartment which they furnished for us at a rate we could afford. It stretched our budget, but we were determined to move. The furnishings were minimal but provided the basics for us and were almost new. The kitchen was small but functional, and all the appliances were new so they worked. The Italian mom taught me how to make some of her specialty dishes and we were over the moon in our new digs.

I quickly made new friends working at the bank. The trust department was like a family and everybody was friendly. I quickly caught on to the workings of the department and enjoyed managing other people's money and assets. Doing the inventory of a new estate was particularly interesting, describing and attaching values to the assets—especially beautiful jewelry. This trust department handled the accounts of many very wealthy people, mostly from the Carmel area. One family I remember, in particular, generated their wealth by determining they could ship lettuce all over the country without rotting, by transporting the produce by truck or train using ice. Salinas was the lettuce-growing capital of California, so finding a method of fresh distribution was a real boon to the growers. This family's wealth was in a trust for the benefit of a son who was too wild and irresponsible to manage the money. He got a monthly allowance from the trust and we paid his bills. Any major purchases he might want to make had to be approved in advance by the trust department. We referred to this as the "ice" account. I was intrigued by this arrangement, but it sure kept their estate intact.

Salinas was, and still is, a major stop on the professional rodeo circuit, so the third week of July was rodeo week. The entire town went "western" and the main street in front of the bank and for several blocks was closed for rodeo-related events. Cowboys and fans swarmed the town and

133

everyone dressed in western wear. I was warned that if you were caught on the streets in traditional dress, you were subject to lockup in the makeshift jail set up on the street. Since I did not own any western clothes, nor the budget to purchase any, my bank family got together and presented me with an early birthday present—a complete set of western wear from the hat down to the boots. Their thoughtfulness and generosity brought tears to my eyes, but how proud I was to strut around town in my new western wear. The week was a time of fun culminating on the weekend with the final championship events in a center specifically built to hold the rodeo. Not much work was done, but there was a carnival, barbecues, and cowboy dances to attend. Regular business took a back seat to the celebration.

Our life fell into a pattern of working Monday through Friday, using the weekend to get together with friends in San Jose. Together we made the trip into San Francisco for Saturday night. My bank family often had home parties to which we were invited, and I had made friends with a local couple who enjoyed showing us the sites within driving distance. Some of the army buddies and their families also had barbecues and get-togethers at their homes or restaurants. Life was good.

I had to save some time on weekends to wash and heavily starch and iron Ken's army fatigues. They had to stand by themselves as a result of the starching. I dreaded this job, but it had to be done. The army required polished boots, shiny brass, and stiff fatigues. It all came to an end one day when the soldiers were told they would be discharged after having served a year. I was not happy to hear this since I loved my job, the people I worked with, and our entire life style. I wanted to stay and my bank friends made all kinds of promises, including a job for my husband, but he wanted to return home. Can you imagine missing Iowa? I often wonder how my life might have been different if we had stayed.

We said our sad good-byes to our new friends and packed our things into our car for the return trip to Iowa. We made our return traveling with our friends from San Jose who were also returning to Iowa for a visit. This trip was in a more leisurely fashion. We stopped in Reno, Jackson Hole, Yellowstone National Park, and Salt Lake City. It was a wonderful trip. We were able to see so many of the country's sites. However, it was still sad for me as I had truly left my heart in San Francisco

My Most Rewarding Career

We returned from our military life in California to our little house in Cedar Rapids, reconnecting with family and friends. Neither of us had jobs and a couple weeks passed by while I was basking in the sun on a lawn chair in our backyard. One day, my husband suggested it was time for me to find a job.

"Me—what about you?"

Never one to be idle for long, I started my search the following Monday.

I submitted several applications and had a number of interviews with subsequent job offers. The one I was most intrigued by and interested in was a shared office between a data processing firm known as National Data Processing Company (NDP) and later changed to Network Data Processing Corporation, and the consulting actuarial partnership of Taylor and Taylor, which later involved other partners. The actuarial partners were also the owners and managers of the data processing company.

I was offered the job as the assistant to the office manager. I quickly learned the job involved a lot of different things—acting as a secretary taking shorthand notes from the actuarial partners, preparing the accounting records for both firms, acting as the human resource director of the company, preparing payroll, and accepting input from commercial clients who were having their payroll or other records prepared in the data processing company. In addition, I would be given algebraic formulas to use in computing premiums, dividends, cash values, and mortality tables for insurance companies—pages and pages of tables to compute for various types of life insurance policies for the actuaries' clients. Oh, how I wished I had paid better attention in my algebra class, never dreaming I would need to know what "x" or "y" meant.

As I became more familiar with my job, my natural curiosity to learn new things took over, and I became interested in some of the data processing functions. The equipment in use at the time of my hiring primarily consisted of key punches, sorters, and tabulators. A new IBM 1401 was being installed in the computer room. It was glassed off from the office area, with special air conditioning, and a raised floor to accommodate all the cables. Everyone was excited about this majestic piece of equipment designed to compute at the snap of a finger.

System analysts and programmers were hired to design and write instructions, known as code, for this

equipment. These programs would take over many of the manual tasks, as well as the tabulating systems for processing data for life insurance companies around the country, as well as the payroll and accounting data for some local companies. Computer operators were hired to run the equipment over a two-shift period.

I became acquainted with most of the commercial customers as they dropped off their data or picked up their reports. The payroll customers were of most interest to me since I understood the process involved. One particular customer was a difficult man to deal with since he always found errors in his reports and would scream and holler at me as if I were to blame. One day he berated me so badly, he reduced me to tears, so I became determined to find a way to eliminate the problems he was having. I developed written input forms and procedures as well as output balancing procedures. I presented this to him the next time he was scheduled and we tried it out. Lo and behold, they worked, his reports were always satisfactory and he told me under his breath— "you're OK considering you're not a guy." I knew there were whisperings about him being gay, but in the early 1960s individuals did not publicly admit it. We developed a mutual respect for each other and remained friends until the day he died.

That also became the start of the company's I/O (input/output) department which grew to be a specialty department for all the systems developed for our customers. I became so familiar with the payroll processing system I was usually the one sent out to sell it to potential customers.

As time moved on, so did the equipment. The company grew, the equipment expanded and was upgraded. IBM was still the primary supplier in the field, but Honeywell was coming onto the scene. I enjoyed meeting the various sales people coming in to the office making their pitches—I called them the blue suits and the brown suits. The IBM

137

salespeople were always in the blue suits, polished from head to toe even with their sales pitches—the Honeywell brown suits never quite measured up although we did acquire some of their equipment. It's strange, but to this day, men in brown suits still do not measure up in my opinion— once I disqualified an orthopedic surgeon I was sent to because he was wearing a brown suit. Interesting how experiences can cause prejudice about such small issues.

As the company grew, so did my position. The office manager I worked under married, became pregnant, and left to pursue other opportunities. I was promoted to accounting manager and became responsible for all the administrative functions. Meanwhile, the systems developed by the company for life insurance companies were being marketed as stand-alone systems all around the country. They were sold and serviced out of Cedar Rapids, Iowa, and produced significant profits. In 1967, it was determined that the company should go public. An in-house attorney was hired to work with me to prepare all the documents and filings for the SEC to make the company publicly owned. What an extraordinary experience and event that ultimately was. This led to more responsibilities and exciting adventures involving purchases of other companies and travel.

The company continued to grow along with my responsibilities. Corporate offices were opened in Oakbrook, Illinois, so I traveled back and forth monthly as Corporate Secretary and ultimately a member of the board of directors. In time those offices were closed and the officers moved back to Cedar Rapids. By this time, I had moved into the position of Vice President – Administration. I was way ahead of my time, since the Women's Liberation Movement was just gaining momentum, but the company president and chairman of the board was very liberal in his thinking, and provided opportunities for employees to succeed regardless of race or gender

I enjoyed the Board of Director meetings held in Cedar Rapids because they were always followed with a "three-martini lunch" at the Piccadilly Tavern in the basement of the Roosevelt Hotel. The chairman of the board always made sure to include me by making reservations in one of the private dining rooms, since women were not allowed in the main dining room. After all, this was a men's club where businessmen entertained their clients and sat around tables drinking alcohol and smoking cigarettes or smelly cigars. This was common because these business lunches were considered a business expense and qualified as a tax deduction. After a lengthy lunch, the directors were sent on their way back to their offices or to the airport to catch flights back home. As incumbent President Gerald Ford said in a 1978 speech, *"The three-martini lunch is the epitome of American efficiency. Where else can you get an earful, a bellyful, and a snootful at the same time?"*

In light of the 2017 news with women accusing men of sexual harassment and other unpleasant behavior, I have to say working in a primarily male-dominated environment, I was always treated with dignity and respect. Yes, there was an occasional pass or lewd remark, but never to the extent of being a serious threat or harmful act towards me. I was fortunate to work with well-educated, professional, and respectful men.

There were many memorable events with the corporate officers. One weekend my husband and I met them after a snowmobile trip we took to the snow mobile test range in the Rocky Mountains. We rode over trails high in the mountains feeling right next to God. We then met the company officers in Vail, Colorado, for a weekend of "meetings," but mostly skiing and partaking of great food in excellent restaurants. This was one of the weekends and trips forever ingrained in my heart as a special experience.

Only we two at the top of the mountain

Sally, Bob, John

Don, John, Sally, Bob

Camping and Boating

Camping as a family when I was young was pretty primitive. As I became an adult and married, we often camped—first in a tent, then we would rent fold-down tent camper trailers, later purchasing a small truck camper, and finally a large very modern truck camper known as a "Swinger." It had all the amenities of a home but in miniature. A group of casual friends camped every weekend at various sites on the Coralville Reservoir. There were enough of us that eventually banded together under the Swinger dealership to form a club known as the Swingers, the brand name of the campers many of us owned.

We became friends with many of the families since we didn't have any children for the first eight years of our marriage. We were able to afford many toys and enjoyed everyone else's kids and their dogs.

We eventually purchased a boat for water skiing and later cruising the Mississippi River with two of the couples we enjoyed the most. They taught us about boating on the mighty Mississippi and camping on the sandbars. At night we would cover our boat with canvas and sleep on the folded-down seats. In the morning we would crawl out, build a fire, and cook our breakfast. There is nothing quite like the smell of fresh-brewed coffee and bacon frying over an open wood fire in the fresh outdoor air. A folding army shovel and a roll of toilet paper accompanied one away from the sand bar to complete the morning activities. A final chore before leaving the camp site for another day of cruising was to clear the area of trash and pick up all our empty cans for proper disposal.

At the time of purchase, this boat had one of the most powerful outboard motors which allowed friends to ski bare-foot behind it on the Coralville Reservoir. It was also built to provide a smooth ride at high speeds over the large wakes made by other boaters or tug boats on the Mississippi. We had many fun days on this sixteen-foot power boat with its 100hp motor.

After our daughter was born, we purchased a small cruiser—large enough to sleep four comfortably with a small kitchenette, shower, and toilet.

Ken and his boat

This allowed us to travel the river for several days, passing through the locks and tying up for the night in various marinas. While pregnant with our son we vacationed on the river, starting in Guttenberg and almost making it to

Minneapolis before returning. During that trip we encountered a terrible storm with rain and high wind on Lake Pepin, the widest part of the Mississippi, which brought water rushing over the bow of the boat. It was scary until we made it to a marina where we tied up until the storm passed. I remember the marine operator telling us we were crazy to be out there in weather like that, since many boating accidents and drownings occurred on that lake which was not deep but wide and treacherous.

Many of our friends would spend the weekend with us on that boat. We usually drove up to Guttenberg on Friday after work, ate dinner at a well-known steak house in town, and spent the night at the dock we rented each summer, heading out early Saturday morning. Guttenberg was the location for Lock and Dam #10, so sometimes we would lock through there to head south on the river, but more often we boated north of town, stopping in Prairie du Chien or heading up to La Crosse in Wisconsin, two of our favorite towns along the bluffs of the river. As we became frequent visitors to the same bars and restaurants in various towns along the river, we became acquainted with the owners. They looked forward to our stopping for a beer or two, or a bite to eat.

Locking through the Mississippi navigation system was an experience in itself. There were rules to be followed, since the river was a primary navigation system for tug boats moving grain, coal, or other products up and down the river running from St. Paul to the Gulf of Mexico. We used our radio telephone to contact the lock master when we wanted to pass through. If the locks were not in use, they would be opened for us. There were stop lights which let you know the status of the lock. If it was in use, you waited your turn idling in the pool below the dam. Once inside, you pulled your boat up to the wall where the lock workers would throw a rope down to you to hang on to while the water level was raised or lowered depending on the direction you were traveling. If

144

you were a frequent visitor to the locks, the workers identified with you and would call out greetings or have a joke to tell you. Most were very friendly and helpful if you had a problem.

Sally and friend

We also got to recognize many of the tug boats pushing barges up and down the river. A friendly toot of their horn was a good reason to smile as you passed them, bouncing over the large wake they made.

On more than one occasion, we met the majestic Delta Queen steamboat cruising the river with its calliope playing and passengers waving at us. That was always a very special thrill.

After our son was born, he would not fall asleep on the boat. His crying at night became so unpleasant we discontinued our trips on the river and sold the boat. That was the end of our camping and boating. That's when we became restless in our current home and began looking for a place in the country.

1969 – A Momentous Year

The year 1969 was a momentous period in my life. Both of my parents were diagnosed with different forms of terminal cancer. They were living in and out of the hospital requiring extra help and attention from my sister and me. On top of that, I was pregnant. We needed to find a bigger place to live rather than in the three-room house that had been accommodating us. We began looking for a home to purchase. After almost eight years of marriage, my pregnancy was a surprise to everyone, especially to my mother who was determined to live until my baby was born, in spite of all the dire predictions from her doctors.

As we viewed house after house for sale, we finally found one to our liking and within our budget. We were sent to the savings and loan company to apply for a loan. By this time, my husband was a sheet-metal apprentice. I was earning the bigger salary at NDP. After reviewing our financial standing, the savings and loan company was willing to give us a mortgage, subject to me signing an affidavit that I would not get pregnant during so many years within the life of the loan. Can you imagine being told that today? Well, that wasn't going to work since I was already pregnant.

We finally found a newly-built Satler Home, wherein the builder was willing to carry a contract for us. I only mention the builder since his sons are now premiere builders in Cedar Rapids and we had been camping friends with the family several years before. Now we were set, or so we thought. We moved into our new house in February 1969. The baby wasn't due until July 25. The company I worked for was going public in September of 1969.

Our first home purchase

On a sunny Sunday on the 29th day of June, friends and family had a lovely baby shower for me. My mother was able to attend, even my maternal grandmother. All my aunts, and most of my cousins and friends were there. We received all the things needed for a new baby. As I was helping to load them into my car, I felt this strange twinge in my back. I attributed it to the three pieces of cake I ate that tasted so good. As I drove home, the strange twinge would come and go. I didn't think too much about it until late that night, when the twinge turned into really awful pains. I finally called the doctor who recommended I get to the hospital quickly. Upon arrival I was hurried to a delivery room where the doctor arrived just in time to deliver a three-pound, two-ounce baby girl. She was so tiny she was whisked away and placed in an incubator, where she remained until the day she was supposed to be born, July 25.

Our tiny 3 pound 2 ounce Lynette

Meanwhile, I returned to work after a few days of rest. We made daily visits to the hospital to view our baby, we couldn't touch or pick her up. She was in isolation because of an intestinal problem that stumped the doctors. In that same hospital, my mother had a room on one floor for her illness, and my father had a room on another floor, each requiring a visit. What a schedule we had.

Friends encouraged us to take the weekend of July 19 off and join them on the Mississippi River with our boat for a couple of days of relaxation and a break from our hectic schedule. This was just what we needed. The next day we were sitting on a sandbar drinking cold beer, when our radio reported that US astronauts, Buzz Aldren, Neil Armstrong, and Michael Collins had landed the lunar module, Eagle, on the surface of the moon. Walking on the moon meant anything was possible, and the space race was on. What excitement this created as we whooped and hollered, raising our beers in the air for a space salute.

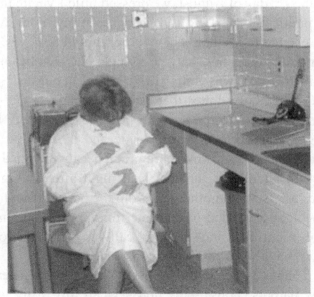

First feeding, nearly a month after Lynette was born

On July 25, I got a call at work from the hospital, informing me I could come take our baby home. She weighed a little over four pounds, which was a surprise, since we were told she wouldn't be released until she was five pounds. I had never even held her from the time she was born. They put me in a swivel chair, gave me a bottle to feed her, helped burp her, dress her, and sent us on our way.

How scary that was to take this little bundle of joy home with no one to really help us. I thank God that one of my best friends came over to reassure me that things would be okay, and okay they were. That tiny little baby is now a healthy, energetic, well-educated, and lovely mom of three children of her own. She is now living the life in San Francisco, where I left my heart so many years ago.

My mother's life was ebbing away. She had been moved to the long-term care facility of the hospital waiting for the day she could meet her new granddaughter. On Saturday, the 2nd day of August, we dressed little Lynette in one of her prettiest outfits and took her to see my mom. Mom was so excited to see her. There were tears in her eyes. She was afraid to touch her, but she thought she was beautiful. We could tell mom was getting tired, so we cut our visit short and returned home. Later that night, the phone rang—we were told to come to the hospital. Mom passed away later that night. Arrangements were made and her funeral was three days later. I write this as important because my dad was too sick to attend her funeral. That night after laying my mom to rest, we got another call from the hospital asking us to come again. My dad passed later that night. Three more days of mourning and another call—my dad's brother passed. What a week of almost constant grief.

Thanks to my mom's closest sister, and a sister-in-law, my parents' house—the house where my sister and I grew up—was cleaned out and made ready to sell. It was the end of a memorable and painful journey. We found a good friend to care for our baby, and I returned to work and doing the things I loved. Life went on. My days returned to normal.

Birth of a Son

I was getting ready for work the morning of February 20, 1973, when I noticed sharp twinges in my back. Ignoring the pains which came and went, we proceeded with our normal morning routines including dropping me off at work this particular day. On the way I suggested to Ken it might be a good idea to head for Mercy Hospital instead. At this time we owned a flower shop that Ken operated. Everybody at the flower shop was happy I waited until after the big Valentine's Day holiday to have our baby. I was glad to oblige, but thought this might be the day.

After being registered and taken to a labor room, nurses did their normal routine and called our doctor to report the concern that the baby was turned, and not in a normal delivery position. Upon arrival and examination by the doctor, he confirmed the baby was in a frank breech position, which made for a difficult and dangerous delivery. Our doctor was a general MD, so he called in a specialist to assist. I was given a drug for pain, and a beautiful baby boy was delivered normally without incident. It was exactly what we had hoped for and now our family was complete. I shouldn't say "without incident" since I had the sorest bottom ever, requiring many sitz baths and a donut cushion to set on for several days.

Coming Home from the Hospital

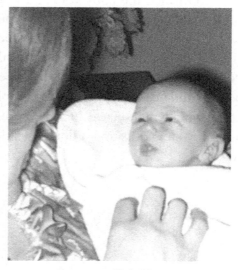

Our sweet little Brent

Brent was a happy baby. He was cared for by a lovely couple who treated him like one of their own while I worked. He stayed with them until our home in the country was finished. Then he went to a commercial day care provider until I was home for a year when he started school.

As a child, Brent's hair was on the blond side and very curly. As he grew older, he insisted on haircuts that kept it very short to avoid the curls.

Brent was active in many high school sports. He especially loved football. From junior high through high school we enjoyed traveling up and down Interstate 80 to conference games. He also ran competitive races from 3K to 10K in length. Cross country was not a school sanctioned sport at that time, but he received many trophies for his efforts.

Country Living

As the children grew, we were ready for a bigger home, preferably an acreage, south of the city, and closer to the Coralville Lake area. We began looking at homes for sale but were unable to find exactly what we wanted. One day as we were driving around, we discovered a new development in the middle of a farm field

This subdivision consisted of one hundred acres plotted into ten lots of ten acres each. Every lot had some timber and rough area. We saw a ranch style home, and we were told the developer had a serious buyer looking to make an offer. The house did not meet all the requirements we were looking for, but the lot next door would give us the land to build our dream home on. After much consideration we purchased the ten acre lot and were given five years in which to complete improvement by building a home. In the meantime, we discovered the buyer of the "spec" home was the owner of the company I worked for—we would be neighbors.

Once we purchased the land, we couldn't wait to begin building. We looked at house plans until we found the perfect house for us, with some modifications. We wanted a split foyer with a walk out on the lower level from the family room and bathroom facing the back yard. We would eventually have an in-ground swimming pool, room for horseshoe pits, a volley ball court, and a vegetable garden.

There would be two bedrooms on the lower level, and three more on the main floor. A three stall drive-under garage would be necessary and two fireplaces—one in the family room and one in the living room. It was exciting planning this home with an architect and our builder. We became good friends with the builder and his wife, since they lived on an acreage just outside the development. We moved into the new house in the fall of 1977.

A view of our country house from the road in the development

A view from the backyard of our country house under construction

156

Finished back yard of our country house

Pool Party

Even sprained ankles didn't stop a game

Ken's Uncle George at the bar-b-que

We loved living in the country, and it was always such a joy to return home to the peace and quiet after spending the day in town. You could feel the air being so much cooler in the summer, just getting away from the concrete and heat of the city. The kids were doing well in the Solon School District and life was good.

Every summer holiday was enjoyed by family and friends, usually numbering around a hundred people. They would play volley ball, horseshoes, swim, or just lounge in the sun.

Some of the seniors would play poker in the shade of the garage. It was always a wonderful day with plenty of food drinks, and fellowship.

Meanwhile, a large management shakeup at the company I worked for was in process, and I ultimately resigned and retired to the country. After many years of being mentally challenged and working long hours, that was quite a change. Our son was just starting kindergarten, so it was wonderful being home with the children and living a quiet life, mowing all that grass, planning the landscaping around the swimming pool, and getting to know the ladies in the neighborhood. However, with both children in school it didn't take long for me to become bored with housework, after all, you can only clean toilets so many times!

An old friend owned a real estate company and asked me to get my license and join his company. Why not, I thought. This would be something new. Little did I realize the difficulty trying to sell homes to people with interest rates in the high teens or in excess of nineteen percent. Financing was almost impossible to get, until some really creative products were developed. This went on for almost five years, when I decided I hated being a Realtor—your life was not your own, people took advantage of you, and it was not my cup of tea.

During this time, I also helped out at our flower shop. I had revamped the accounting system, installed procedures for handling weddings, and put my organizational stamp on everything I could. The only thing I didn't know how to do was the mechanics of floral design. That was easy to fix—an intensive design class was being offered by Kirkwood Community College and I enrolled. I had the artistic ability to design—I just needed to know the mechanics. I was on my way to completing my education as a florist. Of course, scrubbing buckets, care and handling of the flowers from market to cooler, and all the dirty, back-breaking details, were not taught, but I quickly learned in the daily operation.

Sympathy work was historically an important portion of the business and something we excelled at. Local funeral directors were friends and supported us by referring many of their customers to us. We had the opportunity to open a second flower shop in a brand new funeral home being built in a cemetery a few blocks from us. Having a new shop with a drive-in garage for loading, new coolers and equipment, was a dream come true. Business projections for this new shop did not meet expectations, so after only a year we closed it. I had been running the old shop, my husband had been running the new shop, so now it was his turn to go out and find a job, which he did.

Family Matures

Our children, Brent and Lynette now young adults

The kids graduated from high school and after a few false starts went on to lead lives of their own. Our daughter moved to Boston for a year as a nanny and returned home to enroll at Mount Mercy College. She took advantage of a new program being started in the English Department to travel to the Czech Republic and teach English as a second language at Palacky University in Olomouc. She had traveled to Czechoslovakia in 1986 as a high school student, under a home-stay program sponsored by the Czech Heritage Society. At that time, the country was still under communist control. Now that the country was free, the Czech students were eager to travel and to learn English so they could come to the United States.

Lynette Stejskal Cohen and Russel Cohen

Our daughter spent a year in Czechoslovakia, and met a young man from Canada also teaching English as a second language. They fell in love. Upon leaving the country, she returned home. This young man followed her. They spent a year in Cedar Rapids, living in the flower shop house until he was ready to resume his studies. When he entered law school at York University in Toronto, Canada, he convinced Lynette to accompany him and also enroll as a student. She obtained her degree in education there and began working as a teacher in an elementary school.

Graduation day with honors and pride from Mom and Dad

Lynette was married in the backyard of our country home in June of 1993. Her dad built the chuppah out of trees and natural materials from our timber with the canopy covered in fresh flowers. A pair of swans made out of balloons and flowers floated in the swimming pool as a backdrop. Flowers were in abundance throughout the ceremony and reception area. The flower shop staff did a wonderful job in helping with the decorating and creating a beautiful setting. It turned out to be a gorgeous day, considering the year 1993 was a flood year as a result of heavy rains. We were truly blessed since their wedding day was the only sunny day that summer.

Lynette Stejskal's Wedding to Russell Cohen

Our son Brent graduated from high school in 1991, and enrolled in Kirkwood Community College. He was also working nights for UPS and figured out he couldn't do both. He dropped out of Kirkwood and continued to work at UPS until he applied and was accepted into an electrical apprenticeship program under the electrical union. This was much more to his liking since he was always mechanically inclined and preferred the variety of work it provided. After getting a couple of years under his belt, he moved from home and became the proverbial bachelor and party goer until he met "the one." He brought Lisa home, and she eventually became our wonderful daughter-in-law.

Growing up had its ups and downs. We are very proud of the young man he has become. He is a responsible husband and father, and has not forgotten how to do the chores he learned as a child—cooking, cleaning, and laundry. More important, the girl he chose as his wife couldn't be a better daughter-in-law.

Daughter-in-law Lisa Glover Stejskal and son Brent Stejskal

Cigarettes and Pets

Once I learned how "cool" smoking was back in the college years, I continued off and on until I started my full-time career in the software and data processing industry where I became a chain smoker, burning many cigarettes in the ashtray on my desk. I could even fill up the little ashtrays in the arm of the airplane as I flew back and forth from Los Angeles, Chicago, or Philadelphia. It never occurred to me how badly I smelled and what a horrible habit it was, because so many others smoked as well.

As time passed and smoking became less tolerable to society, I began thinking about quitting. It was one of the biggest and hardest challenges I had faced in my life. My husband's employer began a smoking cessation class and offered it to spouses as well as employees, so I decided to give it a try. By then I had been smoking for almost thirty years and was ready to give it up. The class was conducted by a representative of one of the local hospitals. We met weekly.

As the weeks went by people dropped out, so the final class size was quite small. I entered into a competition with a male smoker as to which one of us could hold out the longest. I was determined it would be me. At the end of class we both had quit, and I have not smoked a cigarette since. I later learned my competitor had gone back to smoking, so I really was a winner.

During the early days being around smokers, and particularly my husband, was difficult, but I was determined to beat this nasty habit. There was a lot of complaining to my husband about his continuing to smoke, but it fell on deaf ears. He did try to smoke away from me, and kept his cigarettes in places out of my sight to help me avoid temptation. My husband continued to smoke until he had a heart attack in 2011 and was forced to quit.

I decided to save the money I would spend on cigarettes until there was enough for me to buy something special. At that time in 1991, the cost of a pack of cigarettes was less than a dollar, compared to current prices of over five dollars. I wanted to purchase a Golden Retriever puppy. We adored the neighbor's Labrador and wanted a bigger dog than our Dachshund. Watching the classifieds, I found an ad for Golden Retriever puppies. I called and negotiated the purchase of a female puppy for one hundred dollars. The owners were teachers from New Hampton, Iowa, and they agreed to deliver her to our flower shop one evening. I met them there, and the little bundle of fur was mine to take home. My husband was not thrilled to have a new puppy, but soon became as attached as I. We named her Nikki after the Nicorette patches I used to help quit smoking.

She loved lying on the upper deck of our acreage house, where she could watch over the countryside. When we moved to town we would get phone calls asking if we knew our dog was on the roof of the garage. She had found a way to climb from a picnic table to a storage shed and onto the garage. We decided to build her a tree house in the yard behind the flower shop, which she enjoyed for many years. My father-in-law would come over every morning to coax her up the ramp with a treat, so she could oversee the comings and goings of the world around her.

We had Nikki for almost ten years when she became ill with cancer. She was the perfect dog, always wanting to please, never soiling in the house, or smearing windows, or jumping on people, or doing other annoying things dogs can have a bad habit of doing. She went everywhere with us, including a trip to Canada. We have had two more Golden Retrievers since then, but there will never be another Nikki. That was the best hundred dollars I could have spent from quitting the terrible habit of smoking.

Buying a Weekend Home

We became empty nesters with a huge house and grounds to maintain. After a trip to Toronto for a second wedding reception for the Canadian friends and family for Russ and our daughter, we returned home and decided it would be a good time to put our house up for sale. We received multiple offers right away, one of which we accepted. Now, where were we going to live? With little time to dwell on it, we decided since we had an empty house next to the flower shop, we would clear the storage materials out and temporarily move into it until we decided where we wanted to buy our next home.

Temporary turned into seventeen years, but after living in the country all those years with peace and quiet, the radios blaring in cars, tires screeching to and from the corner stop sign outside our windows, we began to look for a place to get away from it all. There was a place we loved from our early days of camping and boating—Guttenberg on the Mississippi River. We found a lovely house being built as a retirement home by a couple from Dubuque that was located on what was called "The Island" just north of Guttenberg. This couple's needs had changed due to health conditions. They were not going to be able to retire to that location and needed to sell the house.

It was just what we were looking for as a get away from the flower shop and town—a place to rest and relax next to the mighty Mississippi. We owned that property for almost twenty years. It was a great place for our children and grandchildren to visit with fishing, boating, water skiing, and traveling by boat through the locks to other communities for food and beverages. We made many friends there, and as the years went by, lost several of them, mostly to health issues. We spent many holidays there with family and friends

Sandy and Sally bringing in the New Year 2000 in Guttenberg

OUR FLOWER SHOP

"I think owning or working in a flower shop would be so much fun. I just love flowers!" How many times did we hear that over our forty years of ownership. Little do people realize how much work it is designing those beautiful arrangements and all the back-breaking dirty work behind the scenes. You have to love the business and obtain satisfaction from creating something for someone else. I have written some stories to provide a glimpse into the life of a florist.

Purchasing the flower shop meant making application for approval into the premier Florist Transworld Delivery Association. [FTD]. I considered this member-owned cooperative to be one of the best marketing organizations in the United States at the time, as well as the clearing house for sending flowers around the world. Over the years there have been many changes to this organization, as well as a number of other companies entering into the competition of floral and gift giving. However, it is my belief that the marketing efforts of FTD were responsible for the successful floral purchases at Valentine's Day, Mother's Day, and other holidays, as well as everyday occasions not previously recognized as floral occasions.

Purchasing the Flower Shop

My husband's aunt and uncle owned and operated a small flower shop on the southwest side of Cedar Rapids. Originally the business began over ninety years ago as a greenhouse operated by Czech immigrants, my husband's grandmother and grandfather. They grew and sold garden bedding plants and geraniums. Their son, Godfrey, and his wife added the flower shop to the mix which they later relocated to a new facility and home on Bowling Street SW.

They were ready to retire and wanted to sell their business. My husband's mother worked for them on a part-time basis. My husband was finishing his four-year apprenticeship as a sheet metal worker, ready to get his journeyman card.

He came home one day and said, "Mom thinks we should buy the flower shop." I was happy doing what I was doing at NDP, and wasn't really interested. But since my husband always dabbled in artistic things, I agreed as long as it didn't impact me. Silly me—we closed on the purchase at the end of 1970, my husband turned in his journeyman card, and became the proud owner of a flower shop in partnership with his parents.

He soon went off to the Chicago Floral Arts school to hone his skills in floral design, while I was working full time, taking care of the baby, and overseeing the operation of a flower shop. It quickly became apparent to us that his mother knew nothing about being a florist except keeping the floor clean, posting charges to ledger cards, and putting small planters together.

His father continued his full-time job as sexton of the Czech National Cemetery, so he only helped a bit, by watering in the greenhouse on weekends and taking trash out. They had sold their home and moved into the house located with the flower shop so they were on site as a permanent resident. After four years of frustration with this family partnership, we agreed to purchase their share of the business. They moved out of the flower shop property and purchased a small house a block away, from where they could continue to watch over things and help out when necessary. We turned the flower shop house into a warehouse and office. Things were much better after that and family harmony was restored.

We made many improvements to the property, including installation of the sign with message space, and painting the building bright pink.

Life in a Flower Shop at a Major Holiday

Owning and operating a small business provides many challenges. One event in particular sticks in my head. The staff and I were working late the week prior to Mother's Day, preparing for one of the flower shop's biggest holidays. Mother's Day sales were one of our most important financial holidays, contributing the greatest percentage of cash for the year.

Our radio was always on and we noticed the sky was getting dark, when a weather announcement was made for a severe thunderstorm warning with possible tornados. Our rental vans had just been picked up for use over the holiday, since we always needed extra drivers. We staffed the vans by hiring firemen on their days off.

Outdoor flower planters were lined up alongside the flower shop showing their beautiful foliage and colorful blooms. The extra designers had their cars parked alongside the rental vans in front of the shop, since it was after regular hours and our business-owned vehicles were parked under the carport which connected the flower shop and the house next door.

As the wind picked up and it began to rain, the emergency sirens went off and we all huddled outside the back door under the carport watching the storm settle in. The rain turned to hail. It bounced off the cars and stripped the flower pots of their foliage. We stood mesmerized watching the destruction. It never dawned on us to drag the pots under shelter. I also failed to realize the consequences for the business

We were not concerned for our well-being since the flower shop had a small concrete basement and the house next door had a bomb shelter which could be used for safety. After the storm passed, we assessed the damage, which was primarily to the vehicles, flower pots, and building roofs. The rental vans seemed to suffer the most damage, although our employee vehicles also received a great amount. My employees drove mostly newer vehicles, many were SUVs and all suffered several thousands of dollars in damage. I reported the damage to the rental agency and our insurance company, and was shocked to find out we did not have coverage on the rental vans, and we were going to be responsible for the damage.

Shaken to the core by the thousands of dollars estimated in loss on the rental vans, I reached out to our insurance agent to assist me with this matter. With expletives and anger toward me for questioning his lack of concern for our loss, he rudely told me that we would be responsible for the loss. It also turned out he represented the rental agency as well, and they were a far more lucrative customer than my small business.

Meanwhile we still had stacks of orders to fill to make someone's Mother's Day special, so we toiled on. The dollar loss to our business was far in excess of any profits earned for the entire holiday, actually the entire year! That put rocks in the bottom of my stomach and gray hairs on my head.

This was a huge financial problem for me to deal with, but as usual, I pulled up my socks, put on my boots, and approached the rental agency manager to negotiate the dollars down. I was successful in arranging a plan which was agreeable to both of us and a compromise was made. You can bet our attitude towards insurance on rentals changed from no coverage to full coverage. Although there was bad blood between myself and the manager of the rental agency during the time of negotiation, we continued to use their services. She and I actually became business friends during the remaining years we were in business, but I found a new insurance agent.

A Day in the Life of Our Flower Shop

One never knew when you turned that key in the door to the flower shop every morning what the day might bring. You might think you had your day planned, but taking the orders off the printer from wire services, the web site, or answering that first phone call, could change everything.

The first procedure of every day was to unpack, clean and cut all the flowers for placement in sanitized and prepared buckets of fresh water enhanced with preservative. Depending on what came in, this could take a good chunk of the morning's time. Also, depending on which designers were working that day, and the number of deliveries scheduled for the morning, this job often fell to me. It was back breaking and hard work but had to be done properly for maximum shelf life for the products. Some of the flowers might be needed to fill the orders for the day, and would need time to "drink" (take up water into their stems) before using, and before placement in the cooler.

Orders were received for all occasions such as birthdays, anniversaries, get well, sympathy, and any kind of celebration you could think of. Delivering to celebrities visiting Cedar Rapids was always a fun experience. I remember the deliveries to Diana Ross always had to be lavender roses. We filled her dressing room at what was then the Five Seasons Center with dozens and dozens of them. I recall having to deliver to Jon Bon Jovi one day from a besotted fan. I didn't get to meet him, which was okay, since I would not have known him if he was in my cereal bowl. I am not sure we even spelled his name correctly. Other celebrities included John Denver, Alabama, Willie Nelson, Tom Jones, and Barry Manilow. Sometimes it was the event manager calling us from the center, but more often it was the entertainer's business manager ordering flowers in exchange for tickets to the concert. The tickets were generally front row seats. Barry Manilow even came off stage to sing to our teenage daughter. What a thrill for her.

We designed sympathy flowers for many people. A few stick out in memory—the casket spray for a sexually abused and murdered little girl; one for the only daughter of a local dentist who was walking home with a cousin, and killed by a young driver; and the daughter of the community college president killed in a freak accident. Many of these were as emotional for us as for the families we served.

We delivered flowers to many visiting dignitaries and celebrities, but the most famous one of all was a special order for the three presidents visiting Cedar Rapids to dedicate the new National Czech & Slovak Museum & Library.

We were asked to provide a floral centerpiece depicting Iowa and the surrounding area for use in the setting where the three presidents would be meeting. We were also asked to provide flowers for the altar of St. Wenceslaus Church, to be used for a special mass during the presidential visits that weekend. We later duplicated the fresh flower arrangement in silk flowers to be used by the museum as a permanent display in the museum's library.

179

THE BACK PA

Gazette

Presidents leave lasting impression

By Dale Kueter
Gazette staff writer

What's the Secret Service's favorite flower?

Mum. Of course.

And that joke — or preference? — leads the list of miscellaneous highlights that accompanied the Saturday visit of three presidents to Cedar Rapids. To wit:

• Last Thursday afternoon, White House planners put out an emergency call for 100 pots of multicolored mums to decorate the stage where President Clinton, Czech President Vaclav Havel and Slovak President Michal Kovac would speak in dedicating the new National Czech & Slovak Museum & Library.

The Hy-Vee Food Store on Oakland Road NE called suppliers, rounded up 100 plants and delivered them the next

day. The White House used about a dozen. The remainder were kept in the old museum building.

"That's OK," says store manager Gary McClure. "We were just pleased to be called."

The mums, part of a "Three Presidents" display, are now on sale at the store.

• When the presidents held private talks in a corner of the museum library, they sat on black leather recliners loaned by Ethan Allen Galleries. The setting included a $2,000 rug and tables provided by the store.

"I bet we had $10,000 worth of merchandise in that corner," says David Snyder, the store's general manager. The furniture has been returned to the store, but Snyder said he may recommend the setting be given to the museum for a permanent display.

• The floral centerpiece for the presidential setting was created and donated by Stejskal's Florists. The grouping consisted of red carnations, white mums and blue statice. An autumn ensemble included Iowa field corn, small pumpkins and some tiny pigs. Shop owner Sally Stejskal says she's willing to duplicate the live arrangement with silk flowers.

• Jenny Bronstorp, who catered the reception for the presidents, is being deluged with calls for Clinton's menu. People are planning employee Christmas parties, she said, and want to fashion them after what the president ordered.

If that's your plan, here's the menu: pasta salad, couscous salad, smoked pork tenderloin, chicken with leeks, homemade bread and a fruit bowl.

This is the room created for the presidential meeting at the National Czech & Slovak Museum & Library.

180

Newspaper text:
Cedar Rapids Gazette: Wed. Oct. 25, 1995
Presidents leave lasting impression
By Dale Kueter
Gazette staff writer

What's the Secret Service's favorite flower?

Mum. Of Course.

And that joke—or preference?—leads the list of miscellaneous highlights that accompanied the Saturday visit of three presidents to Cedar Rapids. To wit:

• *Last Thursday afternoon. White house planners put out an emergency call for 100 pots of multicolored mums to decorate the stage where President Clinton, Czech President Vaclav Havel and Slovak President Michal Kovac would speak in dedicating the new National Czech & Slovak Museum & Library.*

The Hy-Vee Food Store on Oakland Road NE called suppliers, rounded up 100 plants and delivered them the next day. The White House used about a dozen. The remainder were kept in the old museum building.

"That's OK," says store manager Gary McClure. "We were just pleased to be called."

The mums, part of a "Three Presidents" display, are now on sale at the store.

• *When the presidents held private talks in a corner of the museum library, they sat on black leather recliners loaned by Ethan Allen Galleries. The setting included a $2,000 rug and table provided by the store.*

"I bet we had $10,000 worth of merchandise in that corner," says David Snyder, the store's general manager. The furniture has been returned to the store, but Snyder said he

may recommend the setting be given to the museum for a permanent display.

- *The floral centerpiece for the presidential setting was created and donated by Stejskal's Florists. The grouping consisted of red carnations, white mums and blue statice. An autumn ensemble included Iowa field corn, small pumpkins and some tiny pigs. Shop owner Sally Stejskal says she is willing to duplicate the live arrangement with silk flowers.*
- *Jenny Bronstorp, who catered the reception for the presidents, is being deluged with calls for Clinton's menu. People are planning employee Christmas parties, she said, and want to fashion them after what the president ordered.*

If that's your plan, here's the menu: pasta salad, cous cous salad, smoked pork tenderloin, chicken with leeks, homemade bread and a fruit bowl.

[End of newspaper article]

That was such a huge event. We were so glad to have a part in it that we were quite happy to stand outside freezing our butts off on a very cold day during the dedication ceremony.

There were horror stories as well. One morning the police arrived investigating a stalking complaint by an individual we were making multiple deliveries to. These deliveries were made for a customer coming into the shop, placing his order, and providing his own card message. Apparently the recipient was feeling threatened by the sexually and menacing messages being sent by this purchaser and delivered by us. Once the police became involved, that was the last we saw of this buyer.

A memorable incident involved our mailman, a pleasant young black man who came in one day shaking a package in the air of what he thought were seeds for my father-in-law who was the sexton for the Czech National

182

Cemetery. When he found out the package was not seeds, but remains from a cremation needing to be buried, it scared him so badly, he asked to be moved to another route. Daily deliveries by the postal service, UPS, and FedEx were generally made by the same drivers who became friends with our staff. Some even ate their lunch with us, so we got to know each of them on a personal basis.

Our mailman liked to purchase items he saw in the flower shop for a girlfriend, who also worked for the postal service. A breakup later occurred which upset him greatly. He devised a plan to get her to deliver a registered letter to his son's house, which was on her route and where he was waiting. As she approached the house, he shot her, killing her. He is now serving time in prison. Another driver for FedEx we were fond of would drop in to visit, ended up committing suicide, another incident about which we all felt sad.

One day one of our young designers was alone in the flower shop while my husband was making a delivery, and his mother was eating lunch in the house next door. I did not work in the business at the time, other than keeping the records, so the story was only relayed to me. A male individual came in, pointed a gun at our designer, handed her a bag, and demanded the money in the cash register. She was so terrified, she was clearing all the money from the cash drawer, dropping change on the floor, which he told her to forget as she bent down to retrieve it. He then took the bag and left on foot. Ken returned just minutes after and took off rapidly in the delivery van, looking for the robber throughout the neighborhood. The police were called and the robber was eventually found, arrested, and jailed. Meanwhile the shop lost the contents of the cash drawer in the amount of $185 plus some change. This was a lot of profit at the time. We had one designer very nervous about ever being left alone again.

Flower shops were ripe for the picking with scams and being taken advantage of. We were often used in marital disputes. I remember one in particular where the estranged husband was living with his parents and the wife was living in their home, a family farm west of Cedar Rapids. For several weeks, he ordered expensive deliveries for her which we were happy to provide since they were always paid for by credit card. That is until I received notice from our clearing house that all those charges he made were being reversed, since he was using his dad's credit card without permission. This involved several hundred dollars and was an expensive blow to our bottom line, since there was no way to recover the charges. Apparently other vendors were also involved to the tune of several thousand dollars. The father was a big farmer, well able to cover the charges, but had no sympathy for us, and proceeded to have his son charged.

A final horror story involved our lead designer, my husband, and his mother. They were happily working on a Saturday with everything going well when the telephone rang. The caller proceeded to ask where their wedding flowers were. Oh, no! It was a big wedding out of town by a favored commercial customer, and our staff had forgotten it. Frenzied activity began, things were thrown together to provide as many flowers as could be used, since the specific varieties had not been ordered. The delivery was made. My husband came home that night, a nervous wreck, sure we would be sued, but our attorney assured us that since we had provided a substitute product as best we could in the time allowed, a lawsuit would be without merit. Once I heard about this, I developed specific procedures for weddings and future orders to avoid this ever happening again. A large wall calendar was installed for recording future event orders as they were booked, and each Monday, future work orders were reviewed and moved to the current week daily boards.

Over the years, our drivers could share many stories as well about making deliveries, but that would be a book in itself.

Valentine's Day in our Flower Shop

This was one of the biggest floral holidays after Mother's Day and Christmas. It was one of the hardest because of the limited amount of time in which to deliver the gifts. In spite of the extremely hard work, it was my favorite. Sending gifts of love and dealing mostly with male customers was so much fun. Our greatest concern was always the weather. Timing was also critical as many customers requested delivery during business hours to places where the recipients worked. This primarily happened in just one day, although a few customers would order early.

The first choice in flowers continued to be roses from singles to dozens regardless of price. Over the years, other flowers and gifts were promoted. This holiday has been so commercialized, it has grown considerably over the years. Some have called it a Hallmark holiday since sending valentine cards with messages of love is so popular.

I remember making valentines as a child from construction paper decorated with ribbon scraps, lace, and cut pictures of flowers. They would be distributed at school during a special celebration, usually accompanied with sweet treats. In later years valentines were purchased and carefully chosen for special people with specific messages, and often accompanied by gifts of flowers, chocolates, or jewelry.

Planning for this holiday meant reviewing records from year to year. The day of the week the holiday fell on was important. Mondays were difficult since almost all deliveries were slated for just one day. Tuesday through Thursday were the best. Friday was generally pay day for many of our manufacturing workers, so it was a heavy cash and carry

185

day. Saturday and Sunday were not as good for floral sales, since there was more competition from dining out and other types of celebration.

Flowers were ordered according to designs being promoted as well as estimated rose sales. The best prices were negotiated generally thirty days in advance with brokers located in Florida, since most of our flowers came from Colombia. Some flowers were obtained from national growers, but they were generally not able to meet the demand or competitive price. We had two wholesalers located in Illinois and Minnesota that we regularly used for containers, supplies, and some fresh flowers. They delivered to us on a regular schedule, so we used them on a consistent basis for our needs all year long.

The next step involved scheduling extra designers and delivery personnel. We were very fortunate to have some experienced people who had worked for us over the years and were willing to help at holidays. We were fortunate to get help from the floriculture students at the local community college as well. Firemen were used for delivery, generally the same ones year after year. They knew the procedure as well as their assigned section of the city and surrounding area. Extra vehicles were rented and we were ready for business.

Most orders were taken by phone or received electronically. Because of my experience in the world of computers, we kept our records automated to make orders faster and easier to complete, including point of sale information, card messages, and delivery instructions. No more writing by hand!

After flowers were delivered to the shop, they were cut and processed. Plants were decorated and floral designs were started as many days before as practical. Cleaning and cutting thorny roses was always a hard job. We cut all fresh flowers under water in a special cutter to give them the

186

longest vase life. This prevented air blockage in the stems and provided the ability for the flowers to drink the water, which was specially treated with floral preservative. Our cooler space was limited, so the attached garage was used for extra holding space and delivery organization. Portable heaters were used to help control temperature.

Valentine's Day was a lot of hard work, long days in preparation for it, but a happy and fun holiday. We always provided lunch for all the workers on the day of the holiday, and food for those working through the night before. We had a lot of laughs reading some of the card messages being sent. There were the customers that would spend a long time writing out their cards, tearing them up, starting over, and then sealing the envelopes so their message would be secure. What an interesting experience these wonderful people provided for a happy holiday.

As the daylight faded we breathed a huge sigh of relief. All deliveries had been made, rental vans returned, extra flowers recut and returned to the cooler, the floor swept from all the trimmings which had made everybody in the design area taller. We would fall into bed totally exhausted, but exhilarated from the frenzied activity. We looked forward to the next day's apologetic and forgetful husbands or boyfriends sending their belated valentines.

Our goal was one hundred percent satisfaction for our customers. We worked hard to meet that goal so our complaints were few to none—a great feeling instead of dreading to answer the phone. I loved this holiday!

Design room frenzy.

Taking a meal break on the sales room floor

Deliveries ready

189

Mother's Day in Our Flower Shop

Mother's Day for me is and always will be an emotional day, even before I became a mother myself. My mother was a very special friend to me, always there to listen and always a positive influence.

I took trips with Mom, family members, and her adult friends; learned to play double pinochle with her and the neighbor lady and her daughters; and drank wine with her and many of our other neighbors or friends as soon as I was adult enough to imbibe.

I don't think you ever get over missing your mom, no matter how long she has been gone, if you had a good relationship. Life wasn't easy for her with an alcoholic husband, but I don't remember her ever complaining or feeling sorry for herself, even after being diagnosed with a terminal illness. She made the best of every day right until the end.

I became the mother of our daughter shortly before my mother passed on. Our son was born four years later. These were my greatest achievements. I had been very career oriented and thought I never really wanted children, since my personality was not a warm and fuzzy one. However, holding that tiny baby, totally dependent upon me for its health and well-being, changed my thinking. Right or wrong, whatever you do, has an impact on that little person's development. As a mother, you can only hope and pray your children turn out to be decent human beings making positive contributions to the world. Since I never claimed to be a great parent, I am deeply grateful both of our children have grown into upstanding citizens with wonderful families of their own.

I cannot think about Mother's Day without remembering it as a florist. It was a major floral holiday and the one most dreaded. Business occurred during the entire week before the designated day, and included working on Sunday itself.

Preparation for this holiday began several months in advance. Planning for the perishable products required good record keeping from prior years, as well as searching for new products required for the promoted floral designs. In spite of all the back breaking and bone tiring work required for this special day, the revenue provided a big percentage of the annual income for the business. Our small staff worked long hours for Mother's Day designing flowers and preparing the gifts for delivery by a dedicated group of fire fighters who joined our staff at holiday time to make sure every mom got her plant, bouquet, or gift. This was my least favorite floral holiday since it brought back memories of my own mother when recording the sentiments other sons or daughters were sending to their moms.

This was also the holiday generating the most complaints, not from the standpoint of product quality or service—because our team goal was to get through every holiday without a complaint. The problem was, many moms did not appreciate what their children had chosen to send them—probably wishing for a hug or visit instead. We would hear things like:

"Can I just have the money instead?"

"What am I going to do with this thing?"

"I hate flowers, can I pick something else?"

"Why do they waste their money on something that's just going to die?"

"I'm sure my son or daughter paid good money for these flowers and I don't even like them."

I always had to bite my tongue at the last complaint. I was tempted to say, "No, ma'am, he or she only paid bad money, so try to enjoy them!"

At the other end of the spectrum, many mothers were delighted and so happy to get their delivery. It made my heart

191

feel good when they took time to call to thank us and tell us how much they loved their flowers. I'm sure those sons and daughters were glad they chose a floral gift to send, and so were we.

Even when I was working full time outside the business, I became one of the dedicated volunteers to help at the holiday, along with every other family member, including the children. I remember one particular Sunday, arriving home after the last delivery was completed, excess flowers had been sorted and combined in buckets for storing in the cooler ready for Monday's business, the cement floor swept from all the greens and flowers dropped on the floor as a time saver. We used to laugh about growing at least an entire foot in height at holiday time from standing on the cuttings. Trash was hauled out, delivery tables knocked down for storage until the next holiday, and employees were sent home to spend some time with their mothers.

We would arrive home to our neglected and messy house in the country, with laundry piled high from a week of only going home to grab a few hours of sleep. My feet were so sore and tired I could barely stand, and we were sick of fast food or carry-out eaten on the run. All we wanted to do was collapse in a chair or on the bed and catch a quick nap.

I am always reminded of one particular Mother's Day. As we arrived home my cousin and his wife pulled into our drive on their motorcycle, stating they were out enjoying the beautiful weather and thought they would stop in to say "hello." As I stood in the driveway trying to be sociable, one of them said, "It must be nice to have your own business and rake in all that money." At that point I wanted to smack him and knock her off that motorcycle. Instead, I politely excused myself, told them we just got home and had no time to visit. Maybe they could come another time when it would be more convenient. I turned and headed into the house leaving them to turn around and head back to the road. They had no concept of what we had just gone through, hoping to generate enough money to continue meeting payroll and paying bills until the next floral holiday. I never really enjoyed the holiday until we closed the flower shop and I was free from all the planning and hard work.

Our children always gave me something special for Mother's Day with the help of one of my best friends who took care of them when they were small. As they became adults, they were able to do their own gift choosing. My first really special Mother's Day was spent in Minneapolis with the entire family, including my husband's sister and her family. My niece graduated from college with a nursing degree. We all went to a lovely restaurant for a brunch on Sunday. What a totally enjoyable day that was.

I now look forward to Mother's Day and the special gift and message being sent from my daughter in California, and the lunch, brunch, or barbecue time spent with our son and family—all without flowers!

June Flooding

It's June, the end of the school year. Children will be home and parents will need to find day care for them or things to keep them busy. It was the start of summer and one of my favorite times of the year. The third Sunday in June is Father's Day. Even though it is a national holiday, it doesn't seem to have the same of significance as Mother's Day. As a florist it certainly did not have the commercial importance, although we did have some success with advertised novelty containers filled with plants June 14 is Flag Day, which is not an official federal holiday, but it is so wonderful to see flags displayed by so many people and organizations.

Another significant event happened in June 2008 when the Cedar River flooded the city of Cedar Rapids, cresting at nineteen feet above flood stage. We could not believe what was happening right before our eyes, even though our flower shop and home were not in danger of the rising waters.

On Tuesday, June 10, MidAmerican Energy began terminating the gas service to certain areas along the river. The electrical service was also suspended by Alliant Energy. As the river kept rising, one of our flower shop employees nervously watched the news reports. She finally left to check her home, which was not far from the shop. It was below the hill and in the flatter section of the city, but still several blocks from the river. We were convinced the river would not reach heights to threaten her home, but we were so wrong. By the time she got home, water was already backing up in her basement, so she began moving things up onto the main floor or to the second story of her two-story house. She called me to let me know their situation. They had no relatives in the area, so I offered our small home as a place for them to temporarily stay until the crisis was over.

By the time her husband came home from work, the authorities were evacuating people from their homes, but he was allowed to enter theirs, although he had to wade through waist-deep water in the street. They continued to put as many personal belongings higher than where they thought the water would reach. They packed some clothing, gathered up their dog, and came to our house.

No one would believe the destruction that would occur to our city and the amount of time it would take for people to return to their homes, many of which were totally destroyed including their contents. Even though our gas service was suspended, we were lucky to have electricity. The cable service was a lifeline, since local television networks were reporting the news on a twenty-four-hour basis.

The couple staying with us was somewhat fortunate because the water only rose twelve inches in the first floor of their house. Even so, that required removing and replacing

194

all the dry wall, flooring, furniture, and appliances. This doesn't happen in a few days. Once they were able to enter their home after the waters receded, they worked every spare hour scrubbing, sterilizing, rebuilding, and replacing. They stayed in our home for weeks, but were not displaced nearly as long as many people. During the time of the rising water and news coverage of the devastation, my elderly mother-in-law, living nearby, was a complete nervous wreck, even though she was not in any immediate danger. She did not have television service, which was a serious situation, nor did she have any phone service. We provided her with a cell phone so she could maintain contact with family and friends, but this did not relieve her anxiety.

On the 13th of June, her daughter drove to Cedar Rapids from Minneapolis, packed her clothing and personal things, and took her to their home in Minnesota. This was a great relief for us to have her removed from the tragedy engulfing the city. She remained in Minnesota for several weeks until we felt it would be comfortable for her to return to her home—or perhaps her daughter was ready to move her out. I was not too sensitive to her discomfort since there were so many people that were without homes and all their possessions.

I am writing this in 2016, but I can still recall the rotting, stinking piles of furniture and belongings stacked by the curbs waiting for removal to the city dump—tons and tons of items from people's lives lost to the ravishing waters of the Cedar River.

Once you have experienced this type of destruction from Mother Nature, you can certainly empathize with other parts of our country undergoing similar disasters. We will never forget June of 2008, since parts of the city and surrounding areas are still recovering.

The National Czech & Slovak Museum & Library in Czech Village

The last drive-in A&W Restaurant in Cedar Rapids gone forever

Street after street in the city looked like this

Good Neighbor Day

Good Neighbor Day was promoted by FTD, nationally observed on September 28. It was officially proclaimed as a national day in 1978 by United States President Jimmy Carter. FTD began urging florists to participate in the celebration in 1994 by giving out free packets of roses with instructions to keep one and give the others away.

In 1997 we joined efforts with another florist on the opposite side of Cedar Rapids to promote this special day. We each agreed to give away ten thousand roses, bundled in dozens, to anyone stopping by our flower shops. This was promoted in the newspaper as well as on a popular local radio station. This radio station employed a couple known as Britta and the Bear, who agreed to do a live remote at each of our flower shops.

We negotiated a reasonable price for the roses out of South America, prepackaged in dozens, instead of the customary twenty-five stems. The director and students from the floriculture department of the local community college helped to cut and prepare the roses and place them in buckets of water. We were ready!

What a fun morning we had starting at 7am with people lined up around the block waiting in line to get their free roses. Our little parking lot was jammed with cars. The overflow spilled into the service station next door and into the ice cream shop across the street, much to those owners' dismay. However, since it was still early in the morning, the traffic jam was quickly over.

Britta & the Bear

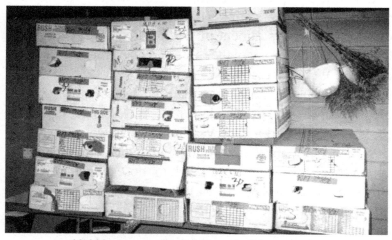

10,000 roses received and ready for processing

Marcia and her crew from the college

Some of our regular staff happy to NOT process 10,000 roses

Good Neighbor's Day at the Stejskal Flower Shop

A representative from our bank, our CPA firm, as well as several friends, helped with the distribution which was complete in less than two hours—ten thousand roses given away to happy people, many of whom we had not seen for several years. Others were just looking for free roses. It was an exhilarating event, a great promotion , but not to be repeated to the same extent in following years.

Closing Our Flower Shop

Age has a way of creeping up on you and after owning and operating the flower business for forty years, we were ready to retire, or at least I was. Aching joints, government regulations over small business, competition from every Tom, Dick, and Harry selling plants and flowers on every holiday and special occasion. That got me to thinking about ways to gracefully get out of the flower shop business. I contacted our corporate neighbor to see if they might be interested in purchasing our real estate, since they already owned two lots directly behind us.

It was a Saturday morning, and I was manning the flower shop while my husband was out delivering. Unless we had sympathy flowers to prepare, Saturdays were relatively quiet. We were only open until noon so we referred to this as our mom and pop time. If things were under control, and Sunday deliveries were covered, we usually headed for our weekend house on the Mississippi River north of Guttenberg. This was our escape from the business and from living in the city. My son and daughter-in-law had stopped by to visit that morning when the phone rang. That telephone call changed the future of our lives.

Several months earlier we had received an offer to sell our property to the business owner next door. We had countered his offer but received no response, so the offer died. My e-mail to the Hy-Vee headquarters mentioned that if they acquired us, as well as the corner gas station, they would have enough space to build a convenience store, gas station, and car wash. The phone call I received that Saturday morning was from a vice president of acquisitions at Hy-Vee. He indicated they were very much interested in talking with us. After some discussion on what price we were looking for, and answering other questions he had, I was told they would get back to us the next week.

Hallelujah, I might be able to retire after all. I was seventy years old and getting tired of running a small business with minimum return and lots of hard work.

Documents were presented for the purchase of our real estate by Hy-Vee, and reviewed by our attorney and accountants. They were finalized and a closing date of February 28 was set so we celebrated our last Valentine's Day.

The real work of closing our business began the day after as we proceeded to empty the accumulation of over sixty years of flower shop merchandise from the shop, greenhouse, garage, and house. What a job! It would never have happened without the wonderful help from current employees, past employees, friends, relatives, and a huge dumpster.

We laughed about the many things we threw away, which were often missing from the dumpster by morning. A huge sale was held. Excess fresh flower inventory, extra supplies, and newer merchandise were donated to the local community college floriculture department, or left for Hy-Vee to absorb into their floral operation.

We signed the final documents in our attorney's office. On the day of closing the check was in our bank account without us ever meeting any of the buyers or their representatives. It was such an easy transaction and we were lucky to own our property and be in the right place to sell it. The end of Stejskal Florist's occurred on February 28, 2011, celebrated by a Mexican lunch and margaritas with all my good employees. It was bittersweet to see shelves empty, but I was looking forward to retirement and new adventures.

Two of our loyal employees clearing the cooler of flowers as a final step in closing for the last day of business.

*Grandma and Blake showing empty shelves,
an empty cooler, and the hand-made closed sign*

203

1937–2011

Out of roses and out of business

RETIREMENT

Retirement means a lot of different things to different people. To me, it was my chance to get off my feet, and do many of the things I never seemed to have time for. I was looking forward to my freedom from running a business. My husband was continuing to work at PMX Industries, Inc., which left me free to plot my course until he chose to quit working as well. I cannot change what life has dealt me, but extraordinary experiences were encountered.

Grandchildren

One of the nicest parts of retirement is the opportunity to have more time to enjoy my grandchildren. They are our pride and joy. Two terrific kids and four wonderful grandchildren, what a great contribution Ken and I have made to society.

Sally and Ken with grandchildren Sydney, Blake, Ethan and Joseph

My Cohen grandchildren

I was sixty years old and becoming a grandparent for the first time. I loved having my children to myself even though they were grown, had left the nest, and established homes of their own. I wasn't sure what my feelings were about sharing my daughter with a new little person who would be the main focus in her life.

My daughter and son-in-law moved during her first pregnancy to San Francisco, California. That is a long way from eastern Iowa, so being a frequent visiting grandma was not to be.

My first grandchild was born October 5, 2001. Sydney Jaye Cohen was a beautiful dark-haired baby girl. Her eyes were dark-brown and almond shaped. When out with her parents, she was often mistaken for an adopted Asian child. We met Sydney for the first time a week after she was born, and immediately fell in love. My selfish feelings quickly melted away after one look, and holding this beautiful baby.

We visited San Francisco as many times as we could schedule into our busy lives and watched this little girl grow. Sydney Jaye was named after her dad's grandfather and a brother, who had both recently passed away.

Later, two brothers, Joseph and Ethan were added to the family, but Sydney was my favorite granddaughter since she was our only granddaughter.

The first of November, 2014, we celebrated Sydney's bat mitzvah. We were excited, honored, and grateful that we were able to do so. This was a totally new experience for us, and we were very much in awe of the religious service on Saturday morning. The evening celebration was equal to, and fancier than any wedding we had ever attended, or serviced, as a florist. We had much to learn about Jewish holidays and celebrations, but enjoyed them all.

The Bat Mitzvah included facts about our universe, and its inhabitants. Prayers were also said for recently departed family members and friends, as members stood and revealed their names. The prayers and actual service was in Hebrew, however the prayer book provided included a translation into English. Throughout the service there was music by a musician, who was a multi-instrumentalist. He did a lot of singing—lines of prayer—and stomping with a tambourine on his foot. The rabbi and community in attendance following along.

The latter part of the service was the Torah service. There was a lot of ritual involved in bringing out the Torah, reading from it, and returning it to the arc where the Torah is stored. My husband and I were called up (asked to come forward to the front) to bring the Torah out, and present it to Sydney. Wherein we then followed her as it was paraded around the room with members of the community touching it with their prayer book, and then bringing the book to their lips.

The Cohen family
photo was taken prior to Sydney's Bat Mitzvah.
From the left: Ethen, Russell, Sydney, Lynette, and Joseph

This was followed by Sydney's fraternal grandparents being called up for an honor or blessing while Sydney chanted her portion of the Torah. There are three of these blessings—one by her maternal grandparents, one by her paternal grandparents, and one by her parents.

As a bat mitzvah, Sydney chose to prepare a story-telling (actually a mini-play) rather than to give a speech, to share the meaning of her portion of the Torah. She wrote a three-act dramatization of her Torah story performed by members of the Congregation. These members were very talented and enthusiastic in bringing the Torah story to our day-to-day life in a way that was thought provoking, moving, and even funny.

After the readings from the Torah, her Uncle Eric lifted the Torah and held it facing the community so all three columns of the scroll could be seen, so everyone knew it was the real deal. He was seated during this part of the service since the Torah is bulky and quite heavy. The Torah was then dressed in its covering, and Sydney's Great Aunt Kathy Stejskal O'Neil helped put it away.

At the end of the service, everyone is invited to the front of the room for blessings over wine—grape juice actually—and bread. This was immediately followed by lunch. The format of the service occurs every Friday evening and Saturday morning. The exception is, it will be personalized on a Saturday morning for a bar or bat mitzvah.

The evening celebration started at 6 pm at a log cabin in the Presidio, which was an army post for 218 years, and is now part of the National Park Service. The theme of Sydney's celebration was Romeo and Juliet and guests were invited to wear Capulet red or Montague blue. The log cabin was transformed into an absolutely gorgeous vision with a canopy of colorful tulle. Beautiful floral designs of roses throughout, including a pedestal candelabra decked in red roses on all the adult tables. Tables were set for adult guests, with a separate area for the youth.

A court jester performed, there was a photo booth, hand decorators painted jeweled designs. A disk jockey, and an emcee kept the party going with dance, games, and prizes. After a delicious plated dinner, a fast moving show of photos from Sydney's life was presented and speeches given by her best friend, her brother, and her parents. This thirteen-year-old young lady expressed her thanks and appreciation for family and friends from there and afar for sharing this special time in her life.

Sydney in the chair lift part of the dance

The remainder of the evening was spent dancing the night away, and visiting with friends and family from Canada which we rarely see. We had a wonderful time watching Blake, our eight-year-old grandchild from Iowa dance.

Blake was the star of the dance floor with unending energy.

It was a time for a variety of emotions, but most of all, a time of enormous pride in this first grandchild and all the many things she has already accomplished in her short thirteen years. We are eager to watch the next phase of her life play out as she applies to high schools in the area, plans a spring trip to Israel and then on to college. With the poise and confidence she already displays, who knows what lies ahead

Our second grandchild was scheduled to be born in July 2004. Our daughter, Lynette, is small framed. Her babies have been over nine pounds so their births have been scheduled for a caesarean section. We arrived in San Francisco a couple of days in advance and were instructed how to take Sydney to school, and then head to the hospital to meet Russ and welcome the new baby, Joseph Leo. When we didn't show up on time, Russ called us to determine where we were. We had missed the freeway exit to the school and were hopelessly lost in the bowels of San Francisco. We were driving a red Mercedes with our grandchild buckled in her car seat in a part of the city we should not be in. Russ gave us instructions back to our starting point and we eventually got Sydney to school and made our way to the hospital for our first look at our newest grandson. That was the last time we were asked to drive anywhere, and Sydney's favorite question was "Are we going the *wight* way?"

Joe was named after my husband's father (Joseph) and mine (Leo) in a special naming ceremony as part of another Jewish custom known as a *bris*. Prior to the eighth day following birth, this was held at home. It is generally scheduled early in the morning so friends and family can attend and still make it to school or work on time. Pastries and morning beverages are served. A *mohel* or ritual circumciser explains what is going to happen, and parents and family gather around while blessings are recited. The circumcision was quick and Joe's grandmother placed a piece of wine-soaked gauze in his mouth to distract from the procedure. More blessings were said and it was time to eat.

This dark-haired deep brown-eyed baby has turned into a very bright young man. He is not the social butterfly like his sister, but enjoys more solitary events and activities. His intellect is far above many young boys his age. His bar mitzvah was an interesting service followed by a wonderful restaurant dinner for selected family and friends that

212

evening. It was not quite the party his sister had, but very enjoyable and suitable for his personality. We look forward to his contribution to society in the future.

Six years later, I received an e-mail picture of an embryo of a third grandchild—another little boy. He turned out to be totally opposite in looks to his siblings. He had a fair complexion, light-brown hair, and a twinkle in his eyes. He was named Ethan Marvel after Babi, Evelyn Marvel Stejskal, the family matriarch who had most recently passed away. We laughed about finally getting a little Stejskal in the family. He is my little guy, youngest of the grandchildren, and growing up quickly.

We were able to attend his *bris* as well. It fell on my birthday, and what a great gift holding this new bundle of joy. He has turned into a very good athlete, loving soccer and snow skiing. He is involved in downhill ski racing and as a seven-year-old won a race against twelve-year-olds,

Ethan Cohen
The stamina of the Energizer Bunny, always on the move.

Joseph, Sydney, and Ethan romping in the surf in New Zealand.

My Stejskal grandson

My only local grandchild is Blake Stejskal was born June 9, 2006. Our son, Brent, and daughter-in-law, Lisa, wanted a baby badly, so her pregnancy was met with much excitement.

Lisa, Brent, and grandson Blake

Because Blake lived close to us, we were able to spend more time with him as he was growing up. From a very early age he enjoyed our greenhouse. [see picture on the back cover.] As he grew he would spend a day at the flower shop when his regular daycare provider was not available. He helped scrub buckets, play in the greenhouse watering plants, or making mud pies, and generally getting dirty. Over

215

the years he made trips with us to our house in Guttenberg. He loved watching the barges and boats go by on the Mississippi river. We were able to watch him grow up and are very proud of his achievements.

Three photos of Blake.   Above with his Dad, Brent

Filling My Day

I looked forward to retirement, thinking of all the things I had been wanting to do and not having the time to do them. The first couple of months were spent adjusting to an entirely different schedule. I still had the accounting records to maintain for the year. The house we moved into the year before had several unfinished projects, but all in all, my new routine began to be rather boring. Our two dogs didn't talk much, and housework had never been my forte.

While I was at loose ends trying to decide what to do with myself, the National Czech & Slovak Museum & Library was preparing for a grand reopening after the 2008 flood. When I received an invitation to volunteer for that opening, I thought, *why not? That sounds like fun!* That became the start of my involvement as a regular volunteer, meeting people from all around the world, and making many new friends. Once again my brain and problem-solving capabilities were engaged, and I couldn't have been happier.

Even though age makes some things impractical, I still want to zipline, jump out of an airplane, and deep-sea dive, but decided one day to try doing some old-fashioned baking instead. I went through all my Czech cookbooks looking for recipes for *zelnicky*. This is a dough similar to a kolache dough, but filled with cooked cabbage and sealed shut instead of an open face pastry with fruit filling. These were a favorite of my husband, and only made by his Teta, Aunt Georgia, who has now passed on. I searched every book until I found the right combination of recipes to make these tasty pastries. I wrote out the directions in great detail, acquired the ingredients needed, and prepared to bake. I started early in the morning after my husband left for work, since this was going to be a surprise for him.

I remember Teta chopped her cabbage by hand, but I decided to use the food processor which was acceptable, but it took me a while to figure out the correct blade so the cabbage didn't turn to mush. That accomplished, I began to fry the cabbage down with an abundance of special seasonings until it was golden brown. This involved a low heat so it wouldn't burn, and lots of stirring, which took quite a bit of time.

While the cabbage was cooking, I started to prepare my dough. Again I looked toward my handy Kitchen Aid mixer. No way was I going to mix that heavy dough by hand. I followed the directions for preparing the dough. I knew one had to be careful with the yeast to make sure it was active, but I had just purchased it so believed it was ready for use. After the dough was mixed, it was time for it to work (which meant rise). I set my oven at its lowest setting to prepare a warm place for the dough to rise, covered the bowl with a dish towel so the dough wouldn't dry out, and placed it in the oven. After the appropriate amount of time, I checked the oven to see how the dough was working. Lo and behold, it was not only rising but had climbed out of the container and was crawling down the sides of the bowl. I scooped all the dough back into the bowl and proceeded with the next step, which meant adding more ingredients and flour to the bowl, beating the dough, and putting it back in the oven to rise some more. This time I watched it more closely as it doubled in size and was ready for the next step. I was getting excited—so far, things were looking good.

The next step in the recipe told me to stir the dough with a wooden spoon. I didn't know why a wooden spoon, but I found one in the drawer and followed the directions, stirring, brushing the top with melted butter, and putting the bowl back in the oven once again for the dough to rise some more. Would this ever end? Time was marching on, and it was now past noon. Finally it was time to shape the dough into balls a little bigger than walnuts. I carefully placed them on my greased baking sheets, flattened the balls, filled them with the cabbage, and pinched the dough over the filling to entirely close them in a bun-shaped ball. They were then put pinched-side down on the baking sheets. Once more, back to the oven to finish rising. Finally it was time for baking.

As I pulled the baked *zelnicky* from the oven with their golden-brown crusts and delicious smelling cooked cabbage, my husband arrived from work wrinkling his nose at the wonderful aroma wafting from those baking sheets.

"Here, try one", I said as I handed him one of the still-warm pastries. I anxiously awaited his assessment. He was frequently very critical of my attempts at cooking.

He said, "They're good—just like Teta's." What a compliment worthy of all that mixing and dough-raising for the whole day.

With my new-found success as a *zelnicky* baker, a few weeks later I decided to try my luck at baking kolaches. After all, the dough and process were basically the same. It was the method for filling and the types of filling which were different. Once again I determined which fillings I would use, gathered the ingredients, and proceeded early one morning to bake again. This time I watched more carefully as the basic dough rose, and proceeded to follow the same directions. Again, this was an all-day process, and as I removed my golden-brown kolaches from the oven, I couldn't wait to taste one. After cooling a bit, I took my first bite—they were hard and crunchy. I don't know what went wrong, but my husband referred to them as hockey pucks, so we fed them to the birds. I haven't had the urge to bake kolaches again. Maybe, one of these days, I'll join the kolache club at the National Czech & Slovak Museum & Library to learn from the pros, or just maybe I'll zipline or try sky diving instead, which sounds like more fun.

Guttenberg: Treasures Remembered

After closing the flower shop, we were not using our Guttenberg home very much since we were finding other interests and places to be instead. I was traveling to visit our family in San Francisco more often, as well as a favorite cousin in Arizona—a great place to go during the ugly month of March in Iowa. One weekend while we were at our " river house," as our grandson, Blake, called it, a new neighbor mentioned his brother was looking for a place to buy on the island. He asked if my husband knew of anyone interested in selling. Deciding to sell our weekend vacation home was a difficult decision, even though our visits were further and further apart. The thought of no longer owning this piece of real estate and having our special get-away place was bringing tugs at my heart and tears to my eyes.

The house was filled with collections of art and my special treasurers acquired over fifty years. What should we do with all these things? Our Cedar Rapids' home was already packed to the brim from our last down-sizing.

Looking around as we were packing our personal possessions, I lovingly wrapped and packed my collection of Golden Retriever plates which were displayed on specially built ledges over the windows in the "all-seasons" room. One by one I had collected them at antique shops, through mail order offers, and flea markets. Each one represented a scene involving beloved Goldens in various stages of their life cycle, or their playful antics as puppies.

Next came the curio cabinet completely filled with pigs. There were pigs of all sizes, shapes, and usefulness—or perhaps really uselessness. What should I do with all these useless pigs? I did have one ceramic pig "puddled out" on the fireplace hearth. There was another gift from a family member, and then there was the antique iron bank pig given to me by a best friend, now long passed. Box by box, the pigs were packed.

Then there were the holiday decorations. All the Christmas trim, the collection of fishing Santas, the tree with appropriate nautical and fishing ornaments and decorations acquired on various travels. All of these made the great room in the house festive and ready for family gatherings and a celebration of the holidays. Oh, what fun we had with family and friends, wonderful food, and huge slumber parties.

As the moving truck was loaded, my thoughts turned to where these special things would be placed. After much pondering, I had it—a great idea. The dog items would be donated to the animal rescue group for their silent auction fund raising. Some of the artwork would be donated to a fund raiser for the veteran flights to Washington, DC. Piece by piece, we were able to store or provide a new home for much of the collections. The treasures remain stored in my mind, safe from destruction, and hopefully available for recall.

Federal Grand Jury

What was this envelope addressed to me from the United States District Court? It sent my heart skipping, but upon opening it I learned I was being summoned as a Federal grand juror to the Court of the Northern District of Iowa. There were a number of documents to complete and return, electronically or by mail, prior to reporting in September 2013. I did not have any idea what being a Federal grand juror involved, but I was soon to find out.

Instructions were given as to date and time to report, where to park, and how to pay for parking. Upon entering the impressive new courthouse recently opened overlooking the Cedar River, I was immediately intimidated by the security system in place prior to gaining entrance to the building. The security officers were expecting us, so we were welcomed through the screening process similar to that at airports. Yes, you might have to remove your shoes and some items are confiscated for the day, like cameras and certain electronic equipment. One gal even had her knitting needles taken away.

We were escorted to a large room designed as a welcome center where we were shown a film and given a brief overview of the federal justice system and the duties of a grand juror. We were then escorted to a court room where twenty-three jurors and five alternates were picked. I was not only chosen as one of the twenty-three, but called to the front by the judge along with two others, and asked if I would be willing to act as a foreperson. I thought she said floor person, but quickly figured out the proper terminology. After the main foreperson, I was designated foreperson #1, and the other fellow as foreperson #2, to act in that order if the main foreperson was unable to be present. I only had to act in that capacity once.

The judge read the specific rights and responsibilities of a grand juror, and we were all sworn in. We were introduced to the grand jury room and related facilities, excused for lunch, and told to report back at a time when my life as a federal grand juror for eighteen months would begin.

Tuesday, Wednesday, and sometimes Thursday were set aside each month, generally during the third week. We were given a schedule at least two months in advance. Our days began at 9:00 am and we were usually finished before 5:00 pm. The days would vary depending on the number of cases to be heard and the availability of witnesses for each case being investigated. Cases could involve drugs, firearms, tax evasion, bank fraud, illegal immigration, child pornography, sexual exploitation, murder for hire, bank robbery, and any other crime against the United States government.

The jury room held the full panel of jurors in courtroom style tables and comfortable chairs, since you spent a lot of time sitting. The district attorney sat at the front along with the court reporter. There was a table with a microphone for the witness being questioned. A full set of audio and video equipment completed the mostly sound-proof room. Personal electronics, including cell phones, cameras, tablets, were not allowed in the jury room. A set of lockers was provided outside the jury room, along with a kitchenette area with a microwave, a small sink, coffee pot, and refrigerator.

We also had a set of restrooms and a locked filing cabinet to hold our notebooks. The notebooks were used for taking notes on each case, and locked away each night before leaving the area. Paper and dividers were furnished for the notebooks. A box of tissue was usually available on the witness desk, not only for the witnesses, but jurors could help themselves as well.

The courtroom staff and security personnel were all very friendly and did everything they could to make us feel welcome and comfortable in performing our service. There was a break room on the second floor with tables and chairs and a number of vending machines available, but most jurors either ate on premises in the jury room, or went out to eat at local restaurants in the vicinity. We had a minimum of one hour for lunch, and often times more before the next case might be ready for presentation. It would have been desirable if there had been a small table and chairs outside our jury room for those eating in or wishing to read using an electronic device, but the jurors' suggestion never came to pass.

The foreperson was responsible for swearing the witnesses in, and if a case was ready for an indictment, reading the charges, asking for discussion and a vote. During discussion on the indictment, the attorney, court reporter, and any law enforcement personnel left the room. A vote of sixteen jurors was required for probable cause to move forward on a case. Some cases were short with only one or two witnesses and could be concluded immediately. Others could run for several months and required many witnesses before being asked for an indictment. At the end of our term, we had a number of cases that did not get presented for indictment. Those cases were passed on to the next panel of jurors.

There could be a lot of time between cases or witnesses, so patience was a virtue. We learned not to expect every case to move along smoothly. After all, we were dealing with criminal cases, so we had to expect the unexpected. Even the attorneys would occasionally have to deal with the unexpected.

With the same panel of jurors meeting for eighteen months, a bond of friendship and respect developed. We each had our own personalities, jobs, and activities, whether active in the job market or retired. We looked forward to meeting each month, eager to learn what cases would be on the docket for the day. We became familiar with the attorneys and learned which ones specialized in certain types of cases. We learned the strengths of each attorney presenting his or her case.

I will miss the monthly sessions and the people involved. It was a real learning experience about our judicial system that I tremendously enjoyed. I am happy I had the opportunity to serve in a capacity I never would have dreamt of doing. I hope everyone notified of possible jury selection will look at it as a positive experience.

Spring Sprung
Summer Shone
Fall Fell
—like a Bombshell

The grass is greening up nicely and growing enough for mowing, my husband's favorite outdoor job. He loves driving his riding mower around our almost-acre lot in the middle of a city block. The daffodils have bloomed and the tulips are getting ready to. The birds are flocking around the feeders and the changing spring ranges from perfect without bugs to miserable with bugs. The trees are starting to bloom or burst out with leaves. What more could you ask for? Then I developed a summer cold, or maybe it was just an allergy with all that pollen. A high dose of vitamin C and lots of orange juice should fix it.

May was a busy month since I co-chaired the museum's annual Taste of Czech and Slovak signature event. It required a lot of planning for the publicity, menu, vendor contacts, and volunteer assistance. It is the springboard for the Czech Village Houby Days celebration and one of the Guild's biggest fund raisers. It is always a big relief when it is over.

I was planning my annual spring trip to San Francisco, only this year was special, since my daughter-in-law, Lisa, and grandson, Blake, were traveling with me. Blake hasn't seen his three California cousins since the Pebble

Beach car show he attended with his dad, Uncle Russ, and cousin Joe the year before, so he was especially excited.

My knees were ready for Synvisc shots (a knee injection to help osteoarthritis) but my medical insurance would not allow treatment until August. I was happy to have family help carrying things and running ahead to our flight gates when time was short.

Our daughter had four days planned in Santa Barbara, so we were all looking forward to sunny days at the beach or resort pool, new restaurants to try, and shopping. This would be a new place to visit, since San Francisco in July is cool and miserable from the fog rolling in from the bay. My son-in-law, Russ, was flying in Friday afternoon to meet us on the beach and join us for an adult dinner that evening at a highly recommended seafood restaurant, the Hungry Cat. Our food and cocktails certainly lived up to its reputation. They offered fresh local sea urchins (uni) which we all passed on, but had a tray of fresh oysters. We coaxed Lisa into trying one for her first time—so proud of her getting it down without incident.

Lisa with her first fresh oyster

227

Our grandson Blake, had never been swimming in the ocean. He was very apprehensive, but it didn't take long before he was romping in the waves and acting very much like a beach bum. The beach at Carpinteria State Park was touted as being one of the safest in the country, without rip tides, and great for kids.

Blake romping in the waves

Little did we know that earlier that morning a shark had been cited eating a seal just off the coast and the beach had been closed. A scheduled training session for life guards had also been cancelled. Since we didn't arrive until midday, things were back to normal and the beach had been reopened. I heard this on the news that evening, so we decided not to tell the children until after all our beach days were over.

We returned to San Francisco Sunday evening while I prepared for a trip with my daughter to take my twelve-year-old grandson, Joe, to Stanford for a debate class he was enrolled in that week. Lisa, Blake, and the other two grandchildren were visiting the wharf and had reservations out to Alcatraz. They were all especially looking forward to this.

Tuesday was departure day, sad to leave, but ready to return to Iowa in spite of the reported ninety degree weather. No matter what, there's no place like home, and I was ready for some rest and quiet time.

My 75th birthday was in September, so a new adventure began in the winter quarter of my life. Remember that nagging cough in the spring? I still had it, so decided I had better check in with the doctor. After a couple of appointments and a chest x-ray, I was told my x-ray was suspicious for lung cancer. This began a series of scans, biopsies, and a Stage 4 diagnosis of squamous cell lung cancer—inoperable and incurable.

My Birthday

August 10, 2016, was a day that changed my life forever when I met with a pulmonary doctor. I was diagnosed with Stage 4 lung cancer, inoperable and incurable. I knew the night before when my primary care doctor called to tell me my x-ray did not look good. I felt like a rock was lodged in the pit of my stomach. Now a new journey would begin for someone so healthy who had never been hospitalized for an injury or illness. Here began the series of pricks, pokes, biopsies, and scans.

My husband and daughter were devastated. My son took the news with the strength of character I would have expected from him. He has been a pillar of support ever since, along with other relatives and many friends. Thanksgiving last year was a celebration of the entire family coming from all over the country to celebrate the holiday with us. I'm sure they thought it was going to be my last one, but so far so good. I plan to be around for another one.

September 20, 2017, was my birthday—a whole year gone by. This one was extra special with so much attention given to me I was overwhelmed. It all started on Monday with exquisite gifts—a hat for my head and a bracelet for my arm. These were right up my alley and chosen by my favorite fashionista. Wearing my new accessories, my sister treated my husband and me to lunch and cocktails at Joe's Crab Shack in Des Moines, my favorite seafood restaurant.

The doorbell kept ringing Wednesday morning with special deliveries—flowers from my son's family, later a loose bouquet from a former employee, a special friend, and a FedEx delivery of tickets for the *King and I* production at Hancher from my daughter and family. My son stopped in the afternoon with a beautifully wrapped Swarovski bracelet trimmed in my birthstone colors—sapphire. Even the landscaper showed up to install the planter around the flag pole my husband ordered for me. How loved I felt.

Wednesday evening involved dinner at the Kirkwood Hotel Restaurant with nine other members of the Floral Careers staff and advisory board. The dinner was provided in appreciation for the advice and support given to the department over the years, and involved a fun time with lots of history discussed and even more in laughs. It was a delicious evening and lasted way past my regular bedtime.

I couldn't help but think of my youngest grandchild turning four and facing his first pre-school celebration on his birthday. He was very anxious about it and came into the family room with this concerned look on his face to ask, "What is a burfday?" After this wonderful birthday, I could certainly answer that question.

The following week I was scheduled for another pet scan after four treatments of Keytruda. This would determine how well this drug was performing and should tell whether there would be another birthday, another Thanksgiving, or more everyday events. Thank you, God, for keeping me upright and breathing air. Fast forward to 2016. Our son had agreed to host Thanksgiving at their home in Lisbon, Iowa. Our daughter and her family from San Francisco planned to visit. Soon we heard my husband's sister and husband were coming from Wisconsin, her daughter and family from Minnesota, another niece and her family from the St Paul area, and one from Pittsburgh with her two sons who I hadn't seen since they were babies. They were now in high school and college. I thought my son would be in cardiac arrest when he found out there would be twenty-five people visiting his house on Thanksgiving Day. It was a good thing my wonderful daughter-in-law stayed calm and grounded.

That Thanksgiving was a wonderful get-together, in spite of the stress for my son and family. I'm sure many of these people arranged their visit for dear Aunt Sally and her recent diagnosis of a serious illness, but what a special day it was spending time with everybody from eighteen months of age to seventy-six.

Left to Right: Kathy, Mallory, Sally, Sandra, Lynette, Lisa. What fun we had when Sally surprised all the girls with shirts designed by folk artist, Marj Nejdl. In Czech they say, "Shit happens," which was Sally's favorite expression after being diagnosed with lung cancer.

231

The Reunion

"Do you think people would come?" I asked during a telephone conversation with a cousin last summer. This cousin lives in Virginia and has one daughter, who is married, and also is living on the East Coast.

"Oh, I'm sure they would," she replied. We ended our conversation with thoughts of a Stejskal family reunion buzzing around in my head.

A few days later, I decided to mention it to my sister-in-law Kathy, and another first cousin Lana. Both thought it was a great idea and agreed to be on a committee to help. We set a date of June 15, 2019, and planning began.

Kathy is a great organizer and immediately began collecting data on each of the family members. There were six second-generation children and their families. Most lived in this area, but a few were scattered around the country. So, this took a while. She was also great at putting together notices and getting them out to people, mostly via e-mail. The response was overwhelmingly positive.

I reserved the hilltop pavilion at Jones Park, so a time and place was established.

A long winter soon turned into spring 2019, and detailed plans escalated for the big event. The caterer was booked, food was ordered, including kolaches for dessert. A room was also reserved at Parlor City the Friday night prior to the big event for a meet and greet.

Let the fun begin!

We had a 95% turnout Friday night, as well as for the picnic on Saturday. Weather cooperated on Saturday and so did the bugs. A quick rain shower kept the temperature mild along with a slight breeze—perfect for a crowd.

Prior to eating, each family was introduced and a picture taken. An ornament was presented to each attending family as a keepsake with the message—"2019 Stejskal

Reunion." It was personalized by my good friend, Marj Nejdl, who is a nationally-recognized Czech folk artist.

Plenty of good food! There were also yard games for adults and older kids, and a children's playground next to the pavilion for those wanting additional entertainment.

The committee was enthusiastically thanked and everybody was happy. Families reconnected. Two brothers who don't speak, actually sat across from each other at a table and talked. It was truly a family reunion.

Back row L–R Brent Stejskal, Sally Stejskal, Lisa Glover Stejskal, Blake Stejskal, Kathy Stejskal O'Neil, Ken Stejskal, Lynette Stejskal Cohen, Russel Cohen, Sydney Cohen with her arm around Ethan Cohen, Joseph Cohen, Brian O'Neil holding Lucy Heger, Mallory O'Neil, with her hand on Audrey, Matt Heger holding Frankie Rose Heger.

Kenneth Stejskal's grandparents
Joseph Stejskal & Agnes Horusicka Stejskal
Their youngest daughter Dorothy is between them
Back row: Ann, Joe [Ken's father] Godfrey, Martha

Winter of Life

Your children grow up, create their own families and traditions, and you find yourself no longer useful to them. The advice they used to seek from you is now being given to you. The visits grow further and further apart, the telephone calls less frequent, and even the grandchildren become immersed in their lives with friends, school, and activities. They have little time for the old people unless forced to visit or spend time. We are mostly ignored until time and circumstances require a helping hand or the required gift for an anniversary, birthday, Christmas, or other special day. Gifting has become a dreaded task, since after a certain age, one has fewer and fewer wants or needs. We mostly appreciate time spent with us or a food gift card.

I must admit we have been lucky. Our children have been very generous over the years. We were sent to Europe for our fortieth wedding anniversary, visiting Budapest in Hungary, Vienna in Austria, and Prague in the Czech Republic. Our fiftieth wedding anniversary was a surprise vacation with the entire immediate family staying in a huge beautiful home in the mountains of Yosemite National Park. A celebration dinner was held in the magnificent dining room of what was then the Ahwahnee Hotel. We have been provided with air fare to San Francisco, tickets to Broadway musicals, weekend get-aways, and many gift cards to places we enjoy eating or shopping. We have been most fortunate!

However, it is a lonely place to be when growing old, no matter how involved in activities you are, and especially when your body no longer allows you to be as active as you would like. I still have many interests, enjoy doing many things, but mostly I love getting the greatest gift of all, having family around. I finally understand how my mother-in-law felt after losing her spouse of over sixty years, and why she often called and worried when she didn't hear from us as frequently as she would have liked. Now I know that feeling, although we try not to be a bother to our children.

Since my diagnosis with cancer in 2016, my mind is busy with a lot of things. My bucket list is running over, and I try to do as much as I can to enjoy whatever time is left for me. I have had many good friends over the years and lost several, have traveled to wonderful places, and enjoyed my family. Do I have regrets or wish I had done things differently? Of course, but that's just part of living and learning. I now look forward to the final chapter of my life, and am planning for the last journey.

Made in the USA
Columbia, SC
20 August 2019